Cosby

COSBY

Ronald L. Smith

St. Martin's Press   New York

Cosby

Chapter

1

"The only thing I had to give him," his mother said, "was plenty of love, and oh, dear God, I gave him all I had. But success comes from within, and Bill was determined to be something."

Born to Anna and William Cosby on July 12, 1937, William Henry Cosby, Jr., arrived at three A.M., just to make sure he had everyone's attention.

He lived in Germantown, a poor district in North Philadelphia. The people who lived there, like the Cosby family, sometimes called it "the Jungle." At first, William Cosby, Sr., made a fairly decent living as a welder, and his family lived comfortably on Beechwood Street. But with an expanding family, ever more pressure, and no way out of long sweaty days and exhausted nights, the elder Cosby began to drink more. The family was washed down to Steward Street and less pleasant accommodations.

There was no bathtub in the house. Instead there was a half-size metal tub that had to be hoisted atop the stove and heated, then lugged back down for bathing. Faced with an arduous procedure like that, young Cos figured there had to be an easier way out. On the nightclub stage, Cosby would talk about bathing in the toilet instead. Of course, he'd warm up the water first—by dumping his brother in it.

As William Cosby, Sr., became more of an absentee father, the family drifted still deeper into the Jungle, ending up in a first-floor apartment at 919A Parish Place in the Richard Allen Homes, a series of squat buildings that housed the poor. The people who lived in them called the place by a less fancy name: "the projects." The homes were among the first experiments in such housing for the poor in Philly. The idea was to file the poor away in neat boxes, as many to a room as they could stand.

Some kids in the projects had a tough time making it home, not because of crime, but because the barracks all looked alike. Every building was the same dirty beige with a stripe of red brick along the first floor. But as Bill remembered it, as bad as the projects were, they could be appreciated as an almost "upper-class place in a lower-class district."

He grew up with the sound of the trains roaring by night and day, shaking the hollow walls and flooring of the Cosby home. "There was a railroad bridge and when Mother would hang clothes the trains would go by and dirty them. But it wasn't a life of poverty. We always had plenty of hot water and heat."

Three more children arrived, one of them an epileptic, and the Cosby household was soon a crowded one. Bill and his young brother James slept in the same bed. He and James shared many of the childhood pranks and jokes that would later turn up in Bill's monologues, from giggling late at night to feuding over who'd roll over on the cold spot when the younger boy wet the bed.

Bill had less time to share with his parents. His mother had to work as a cleaning lady. By the time he was able to say "Dad," he was hardly able to find him anymore.

Squeezed with wife and kids into the cramped quarters at the Richard Allen Homes, William Cosby, Sr., sought a way out. He found it by joining the navy. He also found something else to keep himself out of the house: booze. For young Bill, who thought of his father as "the Giant," and who would later create brilliant humor about the frightening presence of a grumbling parental behemoth, real life was more nightmare than fairytale.

Cos told the story in nightclubs of how he and his brother would wait for their father to come home. He "would go out and really booze it up, 'cause my mother'd give him an allowance of about five dollars and he'd go down to the tavern . . . he'd come home around nine o'clock really loaded." Breathing heavily, struggling with his clothes, he'd drop his pants and the boys would hear the sound of coins.

"Clink! The Giant . . . has money!" And they'd sneak into his room and steal it.

It made a suspenseful story, filled with conspiratorial whispers, the wide-eyed look of fear at being caught, and the glee in counting out eighty-five cents. In the routine, it was even funny when the Giant woke up and said, "Fee, fi, fo, fum, who stole my dough! Was it the kids? I'll beat the kids!" Cosby's mom cried, "Leave the children alone." The

Giant stormed, "Why, you in it with them?" She said, "Yes, I get twenty percent."

Bill Cosby's story, told years later in a nightclub, is more than selective amnesia. It's a magical transformation of pain into laughter. For one thing, Bill's dad rarely came home with any money left over from his nights shooting darts and drinking at the bar. Even on payday, there was somehow no money.

Bill's father didn't *threaten* to beat the kids, but, when his wife pressed too hard for spending money, he didn't bother to threaten. He hit.

A more accurate bedtime scene would show a young, frightened Cos listening with mounting fear and confusion to the strained and pleading female voice and the loud rumbling male voice coming from the other room.

"But Bill, you got paid today!"

"Take this, because that's all I have."

"But Bill—"

"Well, this is all I have, so don't ask me for anymore."

Some nights the loud voices would subside. But other nights, Bill's mom tried desperately to get a share of the paycheck, for the rent, for food, for the kids. And there was the sudden sound of sickening violence, followed by the softer sound of sobbing. Too young to understand and too old to ever forgive, Bill could do nothing about these scenes of anger and tears except hope for the Giant to stay away a little longer the next time he disappeared.

Who was this drunk, violent man named *Bill Cosby?* For the other Bill Cosby in the house, this grown-up image was a source of confusion and pain. *Father.* "The word still spells disappointment to my brothers and me."

Anna Cosby couldn't make it without taking matters into her own hands. With her husband disappearing more and more, she ended up working twelve-hour days cleaning other people's homes, and it still wasn't enough. "Many's the time I saw her come home from work exhausted and hungry and give her supper to one of my brothers who was still hungry after he'd eaten his own."

The family ended up on relief. "We needed those checks on the fifteenth and thirtieth," Cos adds. The Cosby boys tried to make things easier for their mom, but inevitably there would be squabbles, homework problems, or maybe just a game of indoor basketball that left a lamp broken. When there was trouble, poor Mrs. Cosby couldn't help but burst into tears.

"Her tears alone would shake us up," Bill recalls. "No spankings. No beatings. She'd start crying and you'd start crying."

In the midst of the frustration and heartache, Cos couldn't quite understand what was happening. His father was always gone, but now even his brother James was disappearing. For long periods the boy was gone, and when he'd come back, he'd be sick. Little James was only two years younger than Bill, the only other male in the household Bill could play with and count on.

At six, James died of rheumatic fever. The family tragedy only worsened the situation at the house. A few more years, and the Giant was gone for good. He had simply stepped out, abandoned his home and family, and left it to William Henry Cosby, Jr., to take his place.

"My first job," Bill recalled, "was to make a shoeshine box out of orange crates. Then go out and buy shoe polish and washrags and go downtown and shine shoes. When I was eleven, I worked summer vacation at a grocery store. Hauling boxes and stuff, from six in the morning until six at night, nine on Saturday nights. For eight dollars a week. That was 1948."

Not yet into his teens, Cos had three jobs in the fall. First, he had to make money for the family, getting up at sunrise to sell fruit over on Marshall Street, or shining shoes. Then he had school. And then he had to take care of his younger brothers Russell and Robert till his mom came home. He learned to deal with all their familiar childhood arguments, ranging from who got the extra piece of cake left over from last night to when it was time to do homework.

"He kept us in line and whipped us when we got out of line," Russell remembers.

Sometimes it was part of Bill's responsibility to make breakfast. He evidently inherited some skill from his father, who could work wonders with whatever leftovers were lying around—but in the case of the son, there was the unique Cos touch to it. He liked to put food coloring into everything, something his dad never tried in the navy.

"I liked purple waffles, green, orange, red waffles. I loved them and I couldn't understand why my mother never dug them. Nobody seemed to want to eat them. But food coloring is cool. Take scrambled eggs. Put some food coloring in, scramble 'em up, cook 'em, and they look like green or blue sponges."

It was one thing not to eat one of Cos's masterpieces. But not to help clean up? That was something else again. Russell recalls: "I tried to be smart one day when my little brother came out and said, 'Bill wants you to come in and wash the dishes.' I was with a couple of my friends and was going to be real brave and so I said, 'If Bill wants me tell him to come out here and get me.' And he did. It was in the summertime and he put me in this room with no fan, with the windows closed, and he closed the door, and that was my punishment."

Russell would grow into a 250-pound man, and he was big for his age even in childhood, but he never tried to push around his older brother Bill: "I never tried to lick him. . . . I had that father respect for him."

When Cos went to the Mary Channing Wister Elementary School, Bill found himself in the midst of some pretty confusing adults, but at least none of them were as threatening—or as disappointing—as his father. School was weird, though. A curious kid, Cos wondered why, when he was wide awake at eleven in the morning, the teacher would clap her hands and announce that everybody had to go take a nap. He also wondered why the teacher had to know whether he was going to the bathroom for a "number one" or a "number two."

School was a place not to take too seriously, and Cos didn't. Later on, Cosby would look back at ghetto schools and remember them as places of "trouble and turmoil, where the teachers look on it as a steppingstone to somewhere else and nobody really cares and the kids look up to the wrong people." But at the time Cos was doing his best to make it as painless as possible, so there'd be more time for play.

Sometimes Cos would con his mom and get to take the day off pretending he was sick. He found that a little charm could go a long way. "You start out at about three or four conning your mother out of a cookie. You know that she'll say no the first time you ask, but you know that if you can get her laughing you can get around her." Soon he was able to con the teachers and, with a little joking around, con his classmates too.

Nicknamed "Shorty," shy little Cos "got to feeling that as long as people were laughing, they were my friends. So to get myself across and to be an important person, I made them laugh. Through humor I gained acceptance."

Some of the humor came from the unfailing spirits of his mother. Sometimes she would share the humor by spending an hour or two reading funny stories about mischievous boys living down in Missouri.

"My mother used to read Mark Twain to us," Bill remembers. "She scared us half to death with those kids going down into that cave."

To interviewers, who would often ask him about his comic influences, he'd simply say, "Read Twain." He was confident that they would learn something if they did, and even more confident that they hadn't read Twain in the first place.

With young Bill helping his mom to raise baby James, baby Russell, and baby Robert, he probably shared a laugh with her when Anna Cosby would read a passage from a book like *Pudd'nhead Wilson,* where Mark Twain would describe, in vivid picture-perfect detail, life with a newborn babe. Imagine Cosby delivering Twain's lines:

"The baby would claw anybody who came within reach of his nails and pound anybody he could reach with his rattle. He would scream for water until he got it, and then throw cup and all on the floor and scream for more. . . . He was allowed to eat anything he wanted, particularly things that would give him a stomach-ache."

As Langston Hughes wrote, "Mark Twain, in his presentation of Negroes as human beings, stands head and shoulders above the other Southern writers of his times."

But in the public schools of Bill Cosby's childhood, the idea of Negroes as human beings was a novelty. Few teachers sought to instill pride in their black students. However, Cosby remembered one of his teachers, Mrs. McKinney, being very agitated one day. The children at the racially mixed school he attended had just come back from assembly, where they had sung, in about ten different keys, a bunch of songs starting with "My Country 'Tis of Thee." Mrs. McKinney asked the kids if they knew what the lyrics to one of the songs was all about—the one that was called "Old Black Joe."

"She said we were never, ever to sing that song again. She said none of us had any business singing that song. And it brought an awareness to us, because we were just little children and didn't think about what we were singing. But we were absorbing something from that song which said we were second-class citizens."

Cos was learning fast to separate the truth and the lies, and learning even faster how to make his own lies pass for truth. But sometimes he could still get taken in by those adults. Like Mom. Talking about fright and bewilderment onstage, Cos did a riff about the time he was playing with his navel.

"My mother said, 'All right, keep playin' with your navel, pretty soon you're gonna break it wide open and the air's gonna come right out of your body, you'll fly around the room backwards for thirty seconds, land and be flat as a piece of paper, nothin' but your little eyes buggin' out.' "

Cos was so shaken he used to carry Band-Aids in case he had an accident.

Cosby's feelings towards adults in general, and teachers in particular, might best be summed up in a few lines from one of the Twain books his mom read to him. Huckleberry Finn talks about prissy Miss Watson:

"Miss Watson would say, 'Don't put your feet up . . . don't scrunch like that . . . don't stretch . . . set up straight . . . why don't you behave?' Then she told me all about the 'bad place' and I said I wished I was there."

At the Wister School, Cos finally found a teacher who wasn't the typical "Miss Watson." Her name was Miss Mary Forchic. She did her job seriously and joyfully. She knew that the little kids had big problems. They were often hungry, they had to go about in torn clothes and flapping-soled shoes. And they were lost. Lost among all the other kids at school, lost in a crowd of other brothers and sisters at home. And when these little kids were overlooked by adults who considered themselves too big and powerful to give them time or attention, they were not only lost—they were alone.

Miss Forchic's class was for the "unreachable and unteachable" kids, but she felt many of their problems came from their own sense of smallness, helplessness, and lack of self-worth. They needed desperately to have a sense of pride. The first thing she used to do when she set up a classroom was to spread the tables around as much as possible, so each child could have "his own space" and a little breathing room.

Most public school teachers were biding their time, waiting for something better, or simply acting like paid baby-sitters. They weren't about to put in any extra effort to reach out and risk getting kicked by some rowdy brat, or getting yelled at by some obstinate, angry parent who didn't care to be hassled. But Miss Forchic gave her time, and her money. She offered prizes of toys, treated some kids to after-school snacks at the local luncheonette. In order to meet with parents, she would invite herself over after dinner, bringing something for the whole family—dessert.

Cos remembered the time she gave him a special treat. She took him to the movies, giving him a chance to get out of the neighborhood for the first time and see a gaudier, dreamier district of town: "I was so happy to be downtown. After the movie, my teacher took me to dinner and then she rode me home in a taxicab. This was a big thing because in my neighborhood if you rode in a taxicab something bad or something wonderful had happened to you."

"Every child is interested in something," she once said. "The teacher's job is to find out what that something is. If it's baseball or football, for example, you can build math around that." If a kid wanted to know how to compute his batting average, he went to Miss Forchic.

When a child turned in a hastily scrawled little homework assignment, she didn't scream or yell. She said "I'll accept this—if you tell me it's the best you can do." And her techniques for teaching, her dedication and inspiration, impressed Cos enough to make him think about becoming a teacher—a thought traitorously abhorrent to the minds of most kids doing time in elementary prison.

Bill got his first taste of show business in Miss Forchic's class. It wasn't just the way he would cut up for the other kids. Doing that, he'd just get his teacher annoyed enough to warn, "In this classroom, there is one comedian and it is I. If you want to be one, grow up, get your own stage, and get paid for it."

The teacher figured that if Bill was such a natural, why not channel that talent the right way? Bill turned up in such immortal class plays as *Tom Tit Tot* and *King Koko from Kookoo Island.* He loved to perform, but he was still a shy boy needing to be drawn out: "If somebody would pick me for the play I would go ahead and do it, but if they said 'We want a volunteer' I never volunteered."

In 1972, Bill was reunited with his favorite teacher, now the retired Mrs. Paul Nagle of Washington, D.C. At a convention of the American Association of School Administrators, she received an award for her many years of teaching. In an interview for the *NEA Journal,* she shared her advice for teachers, advice that Cos seems to have used in reaching a new generation of kids:

"Learn understatement," she said. "Talk less. Speak quietly. Listen to the children . . . never belittle anything the child says or embarrass him in front of his peers. Instead, help each student to shine in his group."

Cos began to shine a little. Miss Forchic did write on his sixth-grade report card, "He would rather be a clown than a student and feels it is his mission to amuse his classmates in and out of school," but she also noted he was "a boy's boy, an all-around fellow, and he should grow up to do great things."

But how was he supposed to do that, growing up in one of the ghettos of Philadelphia?

Chapter

2

Cosby has tended to sidestep detailed questions about his childhood. Even with close friends, many aspects are "too painful to even think about." Instead, he's created a mythical childhood of laughter with his monologues.

Once, asked if his childhood was a happy one, he answered "It will be, onstage."

Bill's youngest brother Robert put it this way: "Bill could turn painful situations around and make them funny. You laughed to keep from crying."

Christmas was the worst time of the year. It taxed even Cosby's ability to conquer misery with mirth. The stores were swollen with glittering toys, and kids talked about it with narcotic obsession, figuring up the take. In school, Christmas stories and songs painted fantasy pictures of mommy and daddy and the kids having a feast of a dinner and dozens of gaily wrapped presents to give and get.

Some ghetto families risked it all around Christmastime, scrimping and saving to chisel a little piece of that perfect Christmas ice sculpture. But at the Cosby house, with three growing boys, an absentee father, and a mother struggling to keep her family in the projects, some years there was hardly even wishful thinking. The boys knew better than to ask.

At school the teacher would ask if the kids were hanging their stockings on the fireplace. Well, Cos had no fireplace, of course. "We didn't have enough socks for our feet let alone any spare ones to hang."

Christmas was the season when want and need were felt more sharply than ever in the midst of plenty and greed. Only numbing December winds could put a freeze on the feeling of helplessness and rage. It was up to Bill to do something about the emptiness at the Cosby house.

"I wanted to cheer everybody up," Cos remembers. Since they couldn't afford a Christmas tree, "I took an orange crate and painted it with watercolors. We had a little Santa that lit up and I put that on top."

Mrs. Cosby had been working hard all day, as usual. When she got home, there in the corner of the bare apartment was the little painted crate, and the Santa Claus plugged in, the one red light in it throwing off a small reddish glow.

"When my mother saw it—about nine P.M. on Christmas Eve—she put on her coat and went out. She must have borrowed money from the neighbors, but she came back with a kind of scrawny Christmas tree, and the next morning we all had a few presents."

For decades thereafter Christmas would remain one of the most important holidays at the Cosby home, and Bill would try every way possible to avoid nightclub or TV commitments that would keep him away. When Cosby's kids were small, and the family was living in Beverly Hills, the center of attention in the living room was a giant tree, some eighteen feet high, with more presents than its huge, fluffy green branches could hide. It beat out the displays of most of the neighbors, although the tree of silent film comic Harold Lloyd was something special. It was a foot shorter than Cosby's, but Lloyd kept it up—and fully decorated—all year long.

Discussing Christmas now, Cosby's wife Camille says, "I am inclined to give [the children] many gifts because I was given many gifts as a child. Bill is inclined to give them less. He feels that other things are more important. That's probably because he never really celebrated Christmas in that way, because of the circumstances."

What was important was to make every gift meaningful. Once Bill cried because his mom had given him money instead of a real gift. It was just paper to him.

In his adult life, sometimes the simplest gifts have given him the greatest joy. One year, his young daughter Ensa gave him a pair of tennis sweatbands. "He loved it," Camille recalled, "because he knew she had thought 'My daddy plays tennis and likes these . . .' "

As a child, Cos was especially sensitive to gag gifts, or presents that could have been given to anyone. He believed a gift showed how much one person knows about the other, and how much that person cares.

And then there was the black-white problem. Cos remembered the time at Fitz-Simons Junior High when his racially mixed class was celebrating Christmas. As he's often said, he was propelled toward white middle-class values. The radio stars were white, the movie stars were white, and the culture was white. For Christmas, the kids were told to bring in holiday records. One white kid brought a Bing Crosby album. One black girl brought a Mahalia Jackson record.

The class seemed to enjoy Bing Crosby and his "traditional" sound of Christmas. But when the gospel style of Mahalia Jackson was heard, some of the kids giggled, and some of the black kids felt shame. Black wasn't beautiful then, not to see and not to listen to.

Assimilation was as much a battle for Bill as it was for kids of other minority groups. Bill's generation of blacks wanted to be like their radio and movie heroes, and developed the all-American way of talking and walking. Accents, ethnic foods, unusual styles of music were frowned upon. Cosby remembered being embarrassed by his grandparents' accents, where a word like *gentlemen* came out a drawling *jemmen*. Ethnic accents were funny, the kind of thing you'd hear on Fred Allen's radio sketches for "Allen's Alley."

For his junior high friends, Cos would imitate some of the radio comedians, doing a pretty fair squealing Jerry Lewis, and a blustery Senator Claghorn. Radio was a source of wonder for Cos. He was impressed with the way storytellers spun their tales, with the different sound effects and dialects, with shows that had the power to enthrall just with a few vivid lines of dialogue. He loved "Suspense," and "Inner Sanctum," and "Lights Out."

The monsters were special fun. For kids scared by adults and treated like "little monsters," there was a special bond with creatures like Frankenstein's—awkward, ungainly beings who seemed to cause harm no matter what their intentions, and who really only wanted a friend. Their rampages of frustration appeared only natural to the child's mind. They were just tantrums.

In the ghetto real-life crime and fear could be distorted, confronted, and conquered when the villain was something like "The Chicken Heart," the amazing, constantly growing load of pulsating flesh that, in a "Lights Out" radio show episode, engulfed the world and became a vivid memory for Cos. He imitated the show for his friends, adding the sound effects, building up the terror, and then blowing it apart with laugh-making excess. Later, on stage, he went through the process all over again, describing how he listened to the show and got so scared he threw Jell-O all over the floor so the monster would slip if he came through the door.

Hanging out at the apartment of one of the kids who was lucky enough to have a TV set, Cosby saw the comedians up close. He could do their moves, and make funny faces. He used to watch Sid Caesar and Carl Reiner performing on *Your Show of Shows,* and the images stayed with him into the night. "I used to dream of being Caesar's second banana," he recalled.

TV in the early fifties was peopled with friendly comics, stars like Jack Benny, George Gobel, Gertrude Berg, George Burns, and Sam Levenson. Levenson was a precursor to Bill Cosby, a guy who simply came out and told anecdotes about his friends and his childhood. Once a teacher of Spanish in Brooklyn public schools, Levenson had joked with his students and prefaced presentations at parent-teacher conferences with anecdotes and quips. He became an after-dinner speaker, and then a TV star, doing a fifteen-minute show that preceded Jack Benny's. He came out and rapped.

"Good evening, good evening. Relax. It's a warm night and we'll have a lot of fun," Sam would begin, as pleasant as a friendly neighbor. Then on to his observations. "Did you ever try to tell your kid what we went through before anybody gave us a penny? He can't stand it: 'Here we go again. Oh boy, how you suffered.' What's the use of talking to him? Would he believe me if I told him I used to save all week just to weigh myself? And you didn't weigh yourself alone. Who could afford the luxury? Eight kids used to pile on the scale, hold on together, and we weighed ourselves. You divided by eight, each kid got his weight, and we were all happy. I weighed eleven pounds till I was about fourteen . . ."

Levenson even did jokes about his brothers. "We were eight boys. We were born about three weeks apart, we were so close. . . . when my mother hit my brother Albert, I cried. You know why? I knew I was next."

By the time Cos reached junior high, he had bigger worries than getting socked by his mother. He had his hands full with the other kids. Sometimes touch football was tackle. Games with the gang became gang games. There was the time Bill tangled with a lefty named Edward:

"He beat me. I just couldn't get used to a guy with his dukes up on the wrong side. I'd swing to his right and he'd pop me with his old bony left fist. I kept yelling for him to turn around and fight fair."

Kids were restless, sometimes with the kind of restlessness a game of hoops couldn't solve. There were plenty of temptations, and Cos was tempted just like the rest, but he resisted the major schemes and scams because he knew that if he got caught there would be shame and disgrace. If he were put away, there would be Mom, with nobody to look after her except the bill collectors.

Junior high was full of tough kids: "They'd wear the hat sideways, wouldn't stand up straight or nothin', and when they'd talk to ya, they had about twelve toothpicks in the mouth." But they were still just kids. In gym class, half of them didn't know which way they were supposed to wear their jocks.

Some of their favorite pastimes had a ghetto twist to them. Like having fun going on rat hunts in the junkyard. It was almost as much fun outwitting the lifeguard at the public swimming pool and sneaking in for more than the one-hour swim limit, as it was to actually swim. And it was a barrel of laughs to play "buck buck" and have kids jumping on each other, moaning and groaning under the weight as more and more kids would pile aboard.

Cos would later sublimely capture in comedy the childhood glee of rough sport—like in his bit "Revenge," where Junior Barnes smacks him in the face with a slushball. The audience is in tears of laughter watching Cosby, his face a sorrowful pout, cry out, "What you want to hit somebody in the face with a slushball for?" Obviously, for laughs!

Sometimes the laughs were definitely too cruel to be appreciated. In their kid way, some of Cosby's pals couldn't help but be chillingly mean. "Man, you're *really* poor," they'd tell him. They weren't talking about the scuffed, resoled shoes he wore or the faded pants. They were pointing to the eviction notices pinned to his door. And they were glad it wasn't them. Sure, everybody was poor, but look at Shorty Cosby! His family was just this close to getting thrown out into the street.

Even with all the odd jobs he was doing, Cos never quite had pocket money. There were times when he couldn't get dates because of his clothes. The girls took one look at him with his mismatched jacket and pants and didn't look again. He nearly didn't make it to the junior high prom, ashamed as he was of his clothes. To make matters worse, he didn't have money for any transportation except a trolley car. His date's parents took pity on him and slipped him a few bucks for cab fare.

Some of Cosby's friends could make more in sixty seconds of shoplifting than he did in an entire morning of shoe-shining. Even so, Bill felt that he was smart enough to be an honest "con man." He liked conning the teachers, charming the girls now and then, and using some easy jokes and ingratiating gab to coax a bigger tip from the men who asked for a shine.

Mixed with the smile, there was also some resentment about shoe-shining. Bill would call out, "How about a shine . . . fifteen cents." And there would be no response. Then, seeing the guy heading back his way, he'd try again. " 'How about a shine? Your shoes are really filthy . . . a nickel.' And he'd say go. Then he'd give me a thirty-cent tip. . . . It's still the same shine, now what difference does that make? He'd rather have it for a nickel and figure he tipped me a quarter than tip me fifteen cents. How generous of him to do that."

In school he could coax a B-minus out of a C-plus tipping the balance with the Cosby smile. Teachers would just shake their heads. One said, "William, you should be a politician. You lie so well!" Some recognized that he was bright, talented, and something special. An IQ test proved it on paper. He ended up with the tag "gifted," and that meant he could go to a school for "gifted students," Central High School.

Central High had a football team. That was definitely a step in the right direction. Cos remembered how he used to play football out on the street: "We used to wad up newspapers and put 'em inside our sweaters to look like shoulder pads. . . . My uniform was an old pair of corduroys with the torn cuff on the right leg and the shoes with the loose sole . . ."

Now he had his own uniform: good old number 32. He got a chance to learn some real plays, too, on a real field. Out on the street, as described in one of his classic bits, football was pretty messy. The quarterback might offer a play that went: "Arnie, go down ten steps, and cut left behind the black Chevy. Philbert, you run down to my house and wait in the living room. Cosby, you go down to Third Street, catch the J bus, have him open the doors at Nineteenth Street—I'll fake it to ya."

At Central High, it was football the way it *should* be played, with referees and rules and a uniform with protection and padding. What a great environment! Within the first week of practice, Cosby broke his arm.

As for the scholastic end of the deal, Cosby was stifled by the atmosphere of the school, where "gifted" meant cliques of smug, self-assured, and disdainful kids. Cos was out of his depth, and the only thing he could do was demonstrate class-clown bravado, showing the miniature Whiz Kids the difference between uptight and cool.

Cos would be sitting in class, swapping the textbook for a comic book. The teacher would come over, take it, and utter an archly mean-ingful "You'll get this back at the end of the school year."

And Cos would say, "Why? Does it take you that long to read it?"

Cos put it mildly: "I wasn't having any fun and I wasn't passing." He decided it would be best to get out of the place. He went to German-town High, which had a slightly more even racial mix (fifty-fifty), and also kids who were definitely not allowed at Central High: "German-town had some girls at least!"

Germantown High was significantly more comfortable, but by this time Cosby was already way behind in his studies, and he'd lost interest. When he finished tenth grade, he discovered something that he hadn't expected. The *teachers* didn't think he was finished with tenth grade. Left back, Cos found insult added to injury. He was surrounded by babies, kids a full year younger.

Cosby figured he could do better by dropping out and learning a trade. Things weren't quite so bad for the Cosby family by this time. They'd moved to Twenty-first Street, and Cos even had his own room. Now if he took a job, he could keep a little more of the money for himself. Some of his friends were doing all right. They had pocket money, free time, and maybe even a used 1946 DeSoto to tool around in. These drop-outs seemed to have the right idea. Besides, what good was a high school diploma if all you could get with it was a job working in a factory?

Cos apprenticed in a shoemaker's shop, stitching leather soles, tap-ping on rubber ones. It turned out to be a grind, just a dead-end dream. So were the other menial jobs he found. There were still some slick kids Cos knew who were making money the mysterious way—but every now and then they'd disappear. Like from one to three years. "If I do so-and-so and get caught," Cos reflected, "and they lock me up, who'll look out for Mom?"

What else was there? Those futureless jobs? Cosby could hang out in front of his house in the late evening and see the walking dead trudging home somber and exhausted. Their reward was nothing but a cheap meal and a bed and they thanked the Lord for it, too.

Cos thought about it and figured that maybe, for once, his father had had the right idea. Go navy.

Chapter

3

"I joined the navy because my buddies had all joined the air force and I didn't want to be like everybody else."

William H. Cosby, Jr., hospital corpsman, 1956.

The navy promised a chance to see the world. Anything outside North Philly was a new world. Cos spent some time aboard ships from Newfoundland to Cuba and served at the Marine base at Quantico, Virginia, and Bethesda Naval Hospital in Maryland. He was given courses in a variety of medical procedures and ended up working in a ward where casualties of the Korean War lay—many of them amputees, some brain-damaged, others with twisted limbs, all with the dream of piecing at least part of their lives back together.

Some of the patients could even make a few jokes on their tragedies, a line or two about being in the wrong place at the wrong time. Cosby swapped stories about his old neighborhood, and heard ones about the war. Some he would later use onstage, in a graceful balance of humor and exciting storytelling that was right on target, even though it was right on the edge.

He heard of "burial at sea," where the dead are draped in the flag they died for and then chucked off the side of the boat and into the sea.

"It seemed like the cheap thing to do," Cos would tell his audience. "I didn't understand it. I thought the flag was supposed to go with the body. And it must be embarrassing for a guy that dies . . ." The body slides away and the flag is furled back up on deck like some kind of magic trick.

Cosby's imagination took a new twist.

"One of the guys died at sea, and as rigor mortis was setting in we clamped his hands around the flag . . ."

Cos relived the whole scene, complete with the *fudda-dudda-dum* of the sober drums, and the *gobby-hobby domini-domini* of the last rites, and *phew:* the body tumbling over the side, with the corpse's hands clamped tight to the flag.

"Hey, leggo of the goddamn thing—"

"He wants to go with his flag, he loves it . . ."

The stories Cos heard underwent magical changes, and emerged as vivid cartoons that blended comic fantasy with painful reality. He translated battle scenes from the old-fashioned viewpoint of stalwart heroics to the style that would one day become popular with *M*A*S*H*. He had medics realizing they were sitting ducks with the red crosses on their helmets. ("Anybody wanna buy a helmet with a red cross on it? For a gun? How about some morphine? Take this helmet for some morphine.") And he peopled the stage with an entire battalion assaulting a beachhead, the men praying for their lives. He even drew on the forbidden thoughts of self-preservation:

"Medic!" a soldier cries to a corpsman safe in a foxhole.

"Waddya want?"

"My leg, my leg—"

"I don't make housecalls! Take two aspirin and mail in the five dollars."

Cos sounded like a seasoned veteran of combat when he told his stories. But during his navy service, his battlefield was a common one for many blacks. It was just the United States.

Members of the navy track squad, Cos and company would travel by bus to compete with other branches of the service as well as at meets with college teams. He wasn't in the back of the bus on those trips, but once the bus stopped . . .

One day the team bus pulled off the hot, dusty road in a small South Carolina town. The guys piled into the roadside diner, appetites whetted for a fine meal. But Cosby knew that he wasn't welcome. While the others joked around with each other, the black track star walked around to the back of the diner, alone.

He had to keep his emotions under control. But when he opened the screen door in back, he stopped and stared.

The kitchen was staffed by blacks, who greeted him with smiles and soothed the pain by seating Cos down and unveiling the entire well-stocked refrigerator in the white man's diner. The young athlete saw his place of honor crowned with a royal feast of cold cuts, all piled high in a giant hero sandwich.

When Cos got back on the bus, his teammates noticed he was nonchalantly munching on the tail end of a giant hero. Some of them kidded with Cos over his "special treatment," and begged him to let them hang out with him back in the kitchen the next time.

There *was* special treatment in the navy. It didn't have to do with the color of a man's skin as much as what kind of little insignia was on that skin. Cosby took a dim view of the whole system of rank, which made someone better because they had hash marks, or a cap that looked like a bird had gotten sick on it and sprayed it with some mess of gold-colored worms. One stripe made all the difference between an even look into a man's eyes and a forced salute to his power. It was like the ghetto, where the man outside was better. It was like school, where Cos had been two stripes away from graduation and the respect it would bring. And now, with every salute, he was forced to acknowledge a "superior officer."

He looked in the mirror and he saw a man with more tools than most, an athlete with discipline, a man with the brains to be an honor student. Out on the quad he saw the hustlers moving up in rank, moving up in pay, turning around and expecting his salute for their achievement.

By guts and guile, he was determined to change his life. By practice, raw practice, he was getting faster and faster out on the track, reaching higher and higher with his jumps. At work, he was finding ways of reaching the dispirited and beaten soldiers lying in the wards. He decided to "stop fighting things I couldn't change and use the intelligence I was born with." He learned from the men in the wards, and from the guys who were not only bucking for promotions, but getting them.

"I was meeting navy men who really worked at bettering themselves," Cosby recalls, "guys taking college and high school correspondence courses. They were having difficulty with courses that I could do after reading through once. I thought about how these guys were suffering to learn and how much of a sin it was for me, who had a better intelligence, to be doing nothing. I was committing a sin, a mental sin, by not using my brains. So I applied for a special high school program, and got my diploma."

When Cos visited home, he was happy to see that his younger brothers were taking care of business, and the family was doing well. His brother Russell was no longer the mischief-making little kid, but Bill still got a kick out of observing him.

Bill recalled the time he wanted to use the phone, "but my brother

Russell grabbed it first to call his girlfriend. Fifteen minutes later, I listened in and all I could hear was breathing. Picked it up in another ten minutes and heard more breathing. Finally I yelled into the phone, 'I gotta use this phone.' 'You can't,' said my brother. 'We're talkin.' "

Cosby could be pretty paternal even though his brothers were practically out of school. When brother Bob would send him letters, Cosby would read them, then check them for grammatical and spelling mistakes, and then grade them.

Bob knew better than to question Bill's intentions. "With people I love," says Bill, "if they don't do what I think is right, then I become very sarcastic. And that's hard to take. Most of the folks in my family, I think, have this biting sense of humor. If you're out of line, man, they can just drop it right on you. And it's just as dry as sawdust but it just goes so deep into the wound."

In the service Cosby had ripened into a lean six-footer with a wiry frame. Even now, Cos tries to keep it under 190 pounds. Back then he won track awards for the navy team. At the national AAU competition he hit his all-time high of six feet five inches in the high-jump, which landed him a respectable seventeenth place. He could run the hundred-yard dash in 10.2 seconds.

When his four-year hitch was up, he was "too ashamed to go back home and live off my mother," and too proud of his diploma and all the honors he'd won for his track feats. He decided to make a pitch for himself at Temple University.

They were impressed. Heading toward twenty-three, Bill Cosby was more of a man than the freshmen just out of high school. He was a seasoned serviceman, a guy with the guts to discipline himself in both mind and body. Those were the qualities Temple University was looking for. The only thing Cos didn't have was money. But, finally, it didn't matter.

On an athletic scholarship, majoring in physical education, Cos wasn't the stereotypical dumb jock wooed by his school to play ball while somebody else did his homework. In addition to joining the football team and getting his letter in track, Cos maintained a B average in his studies.

Cosby was hustling all over. He was on scholarship, but this didn't entitle him to room and board. He had to commute between home and Temple, which got to be pretty arduous. Sometimes he'd crash in somebody's dorm room, and for meals he'd get somebody to loan him a meal card. Before long he became so well known to the cafeteria personnel that they hardly ever questioned him when he'd walk in.

It was more fun to be on campus. He liked to play drums at jam sessions, and he impressed the girls with his music, his athletic prowess, and his sense of humor, which continued to grow sharper and wilder as he became accustomed to college life.

Temple's athletic director, Ernie Casale, remembers that when Cos came in as a freshman he was all business: "He reminded me a little of the students we had after World War II—they were the best because they came out of the service, and they wanted an education, and they were determined. Bill was the same way. He came to do a job, and he did."

When the freshman came out onto the field, it wasn't to clown around. "Oh, he was a real competitor," says Casale. "In fact as a freshman he was a fierce competitor. He got into a couple of fights, and in fact I can remember him almost being thrown out of a game. That's how much of a competitor he was." In the midst of the rough pushing and shoving of college football, Cos could definitely hold his own. "That doesn't mean he was fighting in every game. I don't recall him arguing with officials or anything like that, but against opposing players in the intensity of the game, he would show his toughness."

Losing wasn't funny to Cos. At least, not usually. But there was the time he was out on the track at Franklin Field with over seventy thousand screaming, cheering fans jammed into the stands to watch the guys from Temple compete against teams from neighboring schools. Cos was the ace of the relay squad, the anchor man, the guy with the powerful kick who could make up ground, put on the pressure, and get the job done.

There he was, primed and ready, pumped up by the roar of the crowd, flexing his muscular legs, kicking at the dirt track and getting ready for the stretch run. On the other side of the track, the relay had begun. Four men running neck and neck, holding their batons, pounding at the cinders so hard Cos could see the flesh on their faces shudder with every stride.

The hand-off to the second team of runners was made, and it was still neck and neck. The runners' eyes burned as they stared straight ahead, arms and legs pumping rhythmically. Now the third hand-off was completed, and, as the runners came around the turn, ready to hand the baton to the anchor men, it looked like it would definitely be up to Bill Cosby to give it the gun and pull out a victory for Temple.

Cos strained on his mark, his arm outstretched just waiting to get the baton. The race was so close the crowd was screaming. In came the Temple runner, chugging furiously. The guy lifted the baton out to Cos and smacked it up against his own thigh, sending the thing hurtling high into the air.

The crowd roared as the rivals got their batons and sped off. Cos stayed on his mark. Ready. But the Temple runner, exhausted and laughing, barely had enough strength to go and get the baton. Chuckling helplessly, he finally picked it up off the dusty track, and handed it to the furious Cosby.

Cos did the only thing he could do: "I took the baton and bopped him right on the head with it, which is when the fans began screaming with laughter. But old Cosby's a team player to the end, and I take off after those runners like a madman.

"I'm running and running, and passing one guy and then another, and then I get what you call rigor mortis if you're a runner. It's from the effort. First my face muscles freeze, then my chest, then my legs. I fall down, a beaten man if ever there was one. And while I'm down, the cat I had hit over the head comes up, takes the baton, and bops me back with it. I couldn't dream up a routine that funny."

Cosby got a nickname at Temple: Riggie. And it stood for "rigor mortis." What with his anchor work on the track squad, his high-jumping, his football, freshman basketball, and shot-putting and discus throwing, he'd tell his coach, "Rigor mortis is setting in!"

But Cos kept going. "If I didn't make good at Temple, I knew what waited for me was a lifetime as a busboy in Horn & Hardart, or work in the factory. I was so afraid that I made myself do well."

As Ernie Casale remembers, Bill's best track event was the high jump. He was the Middle Atlantic Conference champion in that event. "Bill was a very valuable athlete, the type of track man who could get you points in several events. He was the top man in the high jump, but in other events he could get you a second place here, a third place there, getting enough points to help the team. He could play all sports."

In addition to his exhausting schedule, Cos was taking a variety of odd jobs to help support himself at Temple. To reward himself for completing a tough, no-nonsense freshman season, Cos decided to stretch his legs and travel. He figured to see the sights in California and get some kind of summer job. Some kind turned to any kind turned to no kind.

"Well, I got some of the worst excuses for not hiring me," he recalled.

"I got so tired of riding buses and spending money to hear some guy say 'Well . . .' Finally I just called and said over the phone, 'Do you hire Negroes?' 'No.' I wasn't Bill Cosby, famous entertainer, then. I was just a black man trying to get work. And I was ready. If somebody had said 'Burn,' I would have been right there with them. Because the door was being locked. And it was unfair."

Back in Philly, Cos found work, jobs like being a lifeguard at a municipal swimming pool. Returning to Temple in the fall, the sophomore was happy to relax a little, to feel comfortable as a valued, proven asset to the track and football squads. More of the relaxed Cosby humor was showing through.

Most of the coaches had no idea how funny Bill could be. One day Ernie Casale was walking up the tunnel to the stadium for practice when he stopped. He thought he heard his own voice. "And here was Cosby," he recalls with a laugh, "driving these kids wild, imitating me, imitating the football coach, giving a mock lecture, saying things like 'You guys take a good look at this stadium 'cause you'll never see it again.' And this was the first time I'd really heard him in front of a group and he did such a terrific job you could tell that something was gonna happen with that guy. He was great."

There's still a little touch of a blush when the athletic director remembers that Bill's most famous football routine was about *him*. In fact, Cos mentions Casale by name in the extended routine about the Temple squad on his album *Why Is There Air?*

Cosby parodied Casale coming into the locker room before a big game and saying "We wanna keep our television contract going, so remember that you're on TV. . . . You must not touch . . . certain areas of your body . . . when you're out on the football field. . . . If you're out there diggin' and scratchin' people are gonna turn you right off."

There is a resemblance between Cosby's broad impression of Ernie's voice and his natural speaking voice. But, as Casale insists with a little embarrassed laugh, the resemblance ends there:

"We did have a local TV package, because in those days the NCAA didn't package our division and we could do whatever we chose. And it's true, I did go into the locker room, more than one time, and talk to the players about the fact that we're on TV and we want to make a good showing and do things properly. But never"—Casale laughs again—"did I mention what he was saying. He took it from there, and I've always kidded him about that. But that's Bill Cosby."

Cos made the speech into a memorably hysterical routine, climaxed by the action on the field, where, as number 67, his face a mask of comic pain, he gets kicked in the . . . "you must not touch . . . certain areas of your body.' So I grabbed my head! And just to make it look good they took me off the field and bandaged my head!"

Alas, there was also no "nut squad" filled with players running around naked in snowshoes, putting their helmets on backward, and collapsing in front of a priest to pray before going out to get slaughtered by Hofstra. "Oh no," Casale says affably, "the nut squad was a bunch of crap. That was all Bill Cosby again. Every football team has a first and second squad and in those days they were interchangeable."

Two positions on the team were not interchangeable, however, and Cosby was not too happy about it. "They made me a fullback," he once complained. "I wanted to be a halfback. I wanted to catch passes. I was never given a chance to do that."

As far as Coach Makris was concerned, those were the breaks of the game. And the same thing was true of Bill's collarbone after one game. It was broken.

While it's true that Temple was in the building stages with their football team in those days—Casale had arrived in 1959 to help turn the athletics program around—the squad wasn't that bad. And neither was Bill Cosby. Cosby has called himself just "a second-string fullback," modestly adding, "That means nothing. But I was great on defense." Actually, he was good enough to attract the attention of Emlen Tunnell, a scout with the New York Giants. It was unlikely that Bill, several years older than the other college players due to his military service, would have been deemed a youthful enough prospect to be signed, but, as Casale remembers, "He was good. And he could have been a *great* college football player.

"He had the potential. I think if he'd had nothing to do but play football he could've been a hell of a football player." But he was also studying hard for his classes, working out on the track. And there was something else.

During the summer break after his sophomore year, Bill was restless for still more action: "I decided to do something crazy. You know, so I could go back to college in the fall and write a composition called 'How I Killed Myself during Summer Vacation.'"

He got his chance to do something crazy for five dollars a week. A friend got him a job as a bartender in a joint called the Cellar. He was supposed to mix the drinks and tell some jokes, keep things loose and friendly.

Cos put his "con man" experience to work, and he earned tips as the funniest, most charming bartender the place had ever seen. He wrote down jokes he heard on TV, and gags he picked up from the comedy records students were beginning to play, albums by Mort Sahl, Eddie Lawrence, and Orson Bean.

When he felt comfortable enough, he began to stretch out the jokes, building them into bits. But talk about comfort—the Cellar had no stage, so in order to be seen Cos had to do his act on top of a table. And since the ceiling was too low, Cos couldn't stand up to his full height. He ended up doing stand-up sitting down on a chair on top of a table.

When he graduated from the Cellar to the Underground it wasn't a great leap. Both places were in the same building. But at the Underground he was given more time to tell his little autobiographical stories of life at Temple, and anecdotes about the football team. The Underground had a house comedian, an old-timer who occasionally would skip an evening in favor of an extra bottle of booze. Cosby recalls that the guy "went into the tank" more than he tanked up, deliberately missing shows so that the young comic could get that desperately needed experience—and extra pay for a full night's work.

When he got good enough to stand there and do a solid show, he gained even more confidence. His cousin was making a breakthrough of his own, the first black to host a local TV show in Philadelphia. Cos would occasionally go down and try his luck warming up cold sober audiences. They laughed like they were drunk.

Something funny was going on. Not just in Philly, but all over the country. The year before, Shelley Berman had become the first comic to see his record album go gold. Mort Sahl was on the cover of *Time* magazine. Record companies were signing up comics like crazy. An obscure accountant named Bob Newhart, who used to do little monologues over Chicago radio, was signed by Warner Bros. and hustled out to a club to make a record—even though the guy had never faced a live audience in his life. The "new wave" of stand-up comics was making more money in a season than any football player, college professor, or even the president of the United States.

This was the time to go for it, Bill thought.

But as he began making the trip from the Temple track to the smoky nightclubs, from the little TV studio to the classroom, Cos knew something else. If he left school, he might be blowing his career for good, consigning himself to a life in the ghetto forever.

Chapter
4

"**R**oses are red, violets are blue. Grass is green . . . and dirt is brown."

Bill Cosby, beat poet and hip comedian. Playing to the college crowd, Cos peppered his routines with stuff like that. He even used bits from Lenny Bruce albums, telling the crowd he was offering a little salute to Lenny.

Bill wasn't the warm, winning teller of tall tales back then, but then many other comics were also off their marks, just starting out. Phyllis Diller was playing chichi clubs as a hip chanteuse, singing songs like "I'd Rather Cha Cha Than Eat" and telling risqué jokes: "I'm a born highbrow, descended from a very long line—my mother once foolishly listened to." Even Jackie Vernon was a hipster: "I changed my name to Nefarious and wrote things on the wall: The Little Old Winemaker is a Junkie. . . . I pasted peanuts to the windowsill and watched pigeons go neurotic trying to pick 'em up."

Humor at the time was all hostility and intellect. The hot stars were neurotic virtuosi like Shelley Berman and Nichols and May, with their routines about Freud and Kafka, bleeding alone in a hotel room, or trying to pick a casket for a funeral. And there was the staccato attack on the government from Mort Sahl, spoon-and-needle humor from James Komack, racial satire from Dick Gregory.

Cosby tried to fit in. He delivered thought-comedy that cellar bar beatniks could mull over: "A wino drinks from a bottle wrapped in a brown paper bag . . . because he doesn't want to know the end is coming."

He took his bits to the local Philly burlesque houses. He remembers being repulsed watching a faded hooker strutting about "throwin' things, her old filthy underwear and stuff," at the old men at ringside.

The repulsion was mutual. In between dances, he'd get up there, "telling Ivy League jokes to six sailors and a junkie, doing a routine about how Shakespearean actors talk. They didn't want some college darky talking about Hamlet between bumps and grinds, so I got fired."

Cos worked wherever he could, for whatever audience he could find. Using the Mort Sahl ploy, he'd come onstage with a newspaper, or a copy of *Mad* magazine, which was really just a convenient place to tape crib notes on current events and jokes he could use if things got rough.

Cos tried to work before his peers. The young crowd was the most responsive: "What you fear most is an audience of old people. I think we all turn more bitter the closer we come to our own death. Old people are toughest because you don't know how close to death they are upstairs."

But as he mentioned to Rex Reed, he took jobs anyplace: "I went to a beatnik dive—you know the kind—full of ugly Negro girls and ugly white men—sort of a Lonelyhearts integration. But they laughed. I was getting closer. Finally some cat called and said, 'Aren't you the one who does the funny bit about the guy with Saint Vitus's dance trying to light his own cigarette?' I said, 'Yes.' He said, 'I'll give you sixteen dollars a night.' Big Time. What he really wanted was for me to open the joint at seven-thirty before the regular acts went on at ten. Boy, the things they do to you in this business when you are nobody."

Some club owners asked Cos to throw in some filth. A sexy joke here and there. He simply couldn't do it, even though the money was there. For nearly a decade Nipsey Russell had been making good bread telling whiz-bang rhymes to the bar crowd. They'd roar when Nipsey stood up and recited, "I went to see my girl the other night . . . she came to the door in her nightie . . . she stood between me and the light . . . and good God almighty!"

Many black comics worked blue: Russell, Redd Foxx, Pigmeat Markham, even young Flip Wilson did sex and drug jokes.

The other temptation was to be another Dick Gregory. At least Cos could invite both male and female friends to see him if he did a clean act like Dick. Gregory was hot, making big money with racial satire. A new breed, the "white liberal," couldn't get enough of Brother Greg's truthful humor. "Last time I was down South," he'd tell his approving Northern audience, "I walked into this restaurant and this white waitress came up to me and said, 'We don't serve colored people here.' I said, 'That's all right, I don't eat colored people. Bring me some fried chicken.' "

When the laughs didn't come, Cosby experimented with the black-white jokes. They seemed to have enough shock value to bail him out.

During the winter break in 1962, Cos journeyed up to New York. Greenwich Village was the mecca for all the young comics. Cos the competitor wanted to match himself against the best. He could hardly afford the fare from Philly to New York and back, but now was the time to see if he'd ever make the fare by the wages he'd earn in stand-up.

Cosby auditioned for several clubs. One was run by a white Southerner, Clarence Hood. He sat through Bill's monologue and said, "You're hired. Sixty dollars a week."

At the Gaslight, the young black comic tickled audiences with the kind of racial slaps they craved. "I used to live in a nice neighborhood," Cos would tell the bohemians and affluent barhoppers. "Then two white families moved in." Laughter. Applause. The new Dick Gregory.

Other comics watched in jealousy and awe. The raw young talent from Philly had something special. What impressed fellow comics was Cosby, not his material. The key to the success of a comic is the personality. Naturals like Red Skelton, Lenny Bruce, or even Don Rickles can be fascinating even with poor material. As Ed Wynn said, there is a difference between saying funny things and saying things funny.

Cosby said things funny. And he was cool. There was no flop sweat for Cos. While other comics fretted, nervous wrecks, rushing their lines and showing the audience their fear, Cosby took his time. When things were going badly, he could even make a joke of it. One night when the new gags weren't working and the ad-lib riffs were off target, Cos simply curled up out of harm's way and did his show from under a piano.

Offstage, Cosby had to ration his money carefully. He had to make it last, to pay for travel expenses, for meals. The Gaslight's owner couldn't believe that this skinny kid could be an athlete—not the way he was starving himself. To help out, Cos was given a spare room above the club, free.

The comics struggling along with Cosby insulated themselves with the only cloak that could hide their own fears and insecurities: brashness. Some were impossibly hostile, egocentric, and "always on." Cos steered clear of them. But others exposed enough of their sensitivity to allow for mutual note-taking and maybe lunch at Café Figaro, down the street from the Gaslight, where they could talk about making jokes—and making money.

Also making the rounds, unknowns like Cosby, were two former comedy writers, Allen Konigsberg and Joanie Molinsky, now known as

Woody Allen and Joan Rivers. Joan remembered Cosby as a man of supreme confidence on stage. He got the most out of any piece of material. It wasn't a surprise to her when people began to pick up on him. "Cosby went first," she recalled, "Woody popped out after Cosby, Flip Wilson, then me." Of the Village clubs, she remembered "it wasn't all fun. Struggling isn't. A lot of people who recall that time don't remember it as a funny period. But there was so much talent starting out. It was thrilling. Bobby Dylan was on the same bill with me—six dollars a night. He passed the hat same as me. Barbra Streisand. Simon and Garfunkel. Mama Cass was a hatcheck girl. Mel Brooks was a schlock writer then, courting Anne Bancroft. You were just happy and grateful to be working."

Cos was happy to work, and to watch some of the other comics work, like Lenny Bruce. Of Lenny, Rivers recalled: "He saved my life. . . . I watched Lenny's act every night for three weeks. I learned from Lenny that you could tell the truth onstage." Cosby watched Lenny avidly, not only picking up the pleasure of his comedy, but understanding the man's pain. Lenny persisted against all odds. He believed in his style of comedy even when others criticized him and ostracized him. Cosby would soon be blazing his own unique trail of comic style, and he saw, from Bruce, what he might have to face.

"I remember being very very upset that people would come in to see Lenny knowing that he was going to use four-letter words. At that time in the sixties . . . that was really taboo. And I'm sitting in the Village Vanguard—I went to see Lenny because I had all of his records, and the cuts that I enjoyed most had to do with human behavior—and I'll be darned. Lenny started talking, and in the dialogue of the way the people talked, Lenny used a four-letter word. And four people, as if they had been rehearsing this, stood up and said out loud, 'I've never heard such language in my life.'

"And I remember being very, very angry with these people."

Cos could also get very angry and frustrated with his own audiences at times. They didn't get the jokes. They ate and blabbered while he was talking. But he didn't fight them. He knew, even then, one of the basic rules of the comedian: "People have to like you if you're going to be a comic. After a cat establishes the fact that he's funny, forty percent of the pressure is eased up on him because, when he walks out, people already like him."

If Cosby had always kept a firm control on his emotions before, he had to retain that cool in one of the most demanding, and at times demeaning, jobs in the world: that of the stand-up comedian.

Cosby learned that, after winning an audience over, "you have to protect" what you've got. "You can become hostile toward a heckler and people wonder what's happened because you're not supposed to get angry in public."

As with most comics, some of the humor Bill was drawing on was the humor of hostility and anger. There was the tension and hostility of a cynical Noah manipulated by God. There was the frustration of parent-child relationships where the parents are confusing, threatening, and amazingly dumb. There was the short-tempered put-down of posturing karate stars and their smugness. There were lampoons of irritating commercials. In Cosby's case, he effectively turned much of this anger into such pure laughter that the roots didn't show. Audiences laughed when Cos would translate pain into nostalgic humor, like the time he shouted, "Hey, Fat Albert, come here man. This is really groovy. You should see it: Herman's gettin' a beating from his mom. Come on, hurry up!"

But for the moment, Cosby hadn't found the key to translating his personal experiences into that kind of comedy. He was struggling.

Few comics like to talk about the struggle, even from the perspective of twenty years of success. Cos could not only cool his emotions, but freeze-dry them. But another comic starting out at the same time, going through the search for a comic identity and jokes that worked, vividly described what it's like for almost every comedian.

Phyllis Diller, her fist actually clenched as she spoke, said, "It's extremely painful to get there. All along the way people are saying you'll never make it. Practice. Practice is what is so humiliating about becoming a good comic. There's no such thing as a good beginning comic . . . you have a spark and you want to do it, and you have the material and the material isn't that good in the beginning. . . . All of your training is done in front of people and that's what's so humiliating."

Few comedians can bear to go through the pain: "The pain of being lousy," Diller snorted. What's worse, the comic must fight back the sensitivity, keeping just enough to create meaningful comedy, but coating the rest in a protective shell. "All comics are hypersensitive or they could never do comedy," she added. "Well, once you're sensitive, you never change."

Onstage, Cosby would tell the jokes he wanted to tell, then balance them with the racial humor the audiences in the hip clubs seemed to favor. They'd even laugh at an ad-libbed threat: "You better laugh. I've got a club that's the opposite of the Ku Klux Klan."

It had been a cold winter, but Cosby had been warmed by the vague promises of higher wages, and the remembered sound of laughter. Coming into the big time and facing big-time competition, scoring sixty dollars a week, was better than he had anticipated. And he even had a manager now, a guy named Roy Silver, who told him he'd just dumped a singer client on another manager so he could concentrate on Cos. The singer that Silver let go was somebody named Bobby Dylan.

At Temple, Cos paid less and less attention to his studies. All he could think about was comedy routines. His mother watched and worried. If he got thrown out of Temple, what would he do?

Cos couldn't think about the one-in-a-million shot at becoming a pro football player. He couldn't think about the books and the tests the professors were bugging him with. He wanted to get back to the Gaslight. It looked like his future was there.

Chapter
5

Could you imagine the first black president of the United States? Cos imagined the glorious day—and told his audiences he could just see the response. For Sale signs in the yards of every home up and down Pennsylvania Avenue.

With barely a few sporadic years of experience, Cosby was attracting the attention of the big shots. *The New York Times* did a piece on the unknown comic, and in bold type they enthused, PHILADELPHIA NEGRO AIMS HIS BARBS AT RACE RELATIONS.

They praised young Bill Cosby for "hurling verbal spears at the relations between whites and Negroes," and for staying in college: "Besides verbal spears, Mr. Cosby throws the discus and javelin, broad-jumps, high-jumps, runs the 200-low hurdles, and plays right halfback on Temple's football team."

The professional verdict was that "his output thus far is limited, his viewpoint is fresh, slightly ironic, and his best quips are extremely funny."

In the summer of 1962 Cos saw his salary doubled, and the Gaslight extended him on and on, week after week, giving him more and more chances to hone his craft. He'd go up on the stage and do a quick ten minutes when he felt he had something new, otherwise he'd hang out in the coffee shops, play a few rounds of hoops at the basketball court down on Sixth Avenue, or study tapes of his show in his little room above the club.

Earlier, he had studied other people's records: ones by Lenny Bruce, Reiner and Brooks, and Brother Dave Gardner. "Just as some people might learn songs, I'd memorize comedy routines." Now came a more difficult time, when he had to listen to his own stuff over and over, correct the mistakes, and move ahead.

"At that time," he recalls, "there was no Fat Albert or any of the other characters. I was basically doing sociopolitical material, learning to be a stand-up comic. You cannot learn to do that at home. You have to find an audience to talk to in order to get laughs. That's what I was trying to do. It was at the Gaslight that the 'Noah and the Ark' routine was developed and finished."

Cosby's salary hit two hundred dollars a week. His confidence and drive were at an all-time high. To reporter Hans Knight, Cos was very specific about his goals. "If you asked me why I'm in this, I'd have to tell you honestly—for the money. Yes, sure, I like the work. But I'm not fooling myself or anybody else. I don't consider myself an artist who has to do this because he can't help himself. I think I am funny. I see things funny and I talk about the way I see them. I try to project a family atmosphere—intimate, like sharing a joke with your friends or relatives in your home." And, cautiously, "If I fail I can always go back to Philadelphia . . ."

Now the idea of taking up some other profession was dim. The thought of going back to school was a hindrance. How could he quit when he was on a roll?

With his natural cool, and his collection of racial quips, he was more comfortable onstage than ever. He'd learned by trial and error how to handle the crowds. Once, when a table of ringsiders were distracting him by their double-O staring eyes and stony expressions, he simply slid down off the stage, sat at the table with them, and told his jokes from there. He coaxed the smiles out of them, and developed one more weapon. Years later, it would become standard Cosby procedure to warm up the crowd with ringsider conversation, opening slow and easy, winning friends immediately.

Some weeks no money came in. Some weeks the take varied from a two-hundred-dollar high to a seventy-five-dollar one-nighter low. At least the *New York Times* clipping helped. Cos had to admire Roy Silver for that. Roy recalled pumping the *Times* writer so full of drinks he could hardly slosh out of the club . . . and it was with Silver's help that he managed to come up with such a positive (and coherent) review the following day.

Cos didn't need a manager the way some comics did. Woody Allen needed a manager to literally shove him onstage. Even then, Woody would shield his eyes from the spotlight, hunch over in a crouch, or turn around and do his jokes to the back wall. Cosby, on the other hand, needed someone to help get the bookings, and to help formulate a plan of attack. Just a few years older than Cosby at twenty-nine, Roy Silver looked like an unlikely partner in such an attack. He seemed like any other white Ivy Leaguer, with his studious black glasses and close-cropped hair. He looked like somebody's accountant. In fact, before hooking up with Bob Dylan and Mama Cass Elliot, he had worked as director of research for the Scientific Design Company.

Now he and Cosby worked on making sure Bill had enough surefire material to keep him going strong night after night, place after place, and again when he got those return bookings.

It meant more hard work. "People are always saying to me today that Bill is where he is because he's lucky. There's some kind of magic, you see. You've got it and that's it, people laugh. Oh, boy! Bill would do six shows a night, and I'd sit at each one with a tape recorder, getting down every word and every reaction from the audience. After the last show, we'd go up to my dump or his and spend all night sweating about every line. Thus and such was funny in the first two shows, but not the others. Why not? Didn't you punch it right? Was your timing off? Was it just a dead audience? Line by line like this for weeks, till we knew we had a thirty-minute set that was working."

It was tedious work, as Silver recalls, to "go over every single line, edit and cut, edit and cut," paying attention to a phrase, to a misplaced adjective, making the lines flow like poetry. The two men had fights. Long hot summer nights brought tension. Being "almost there" brought frustration.

There was yet another problem, one that both Bill and Roy Silver recognized. Bill was rebelling against the "Negro comedian" tag. He didn't like doing all those race jokes. It wasn't him. It wasn't the kind of comedy he was best at, even if it seemed to go over well in the hard, hip Village clubs. For Silver, there was the Catch-22 of booking his client as another Dick Gregory, and then finding people cooling off because they thought he was . . . just another Dick Gregory.

"I found that, to be a success," Cos recalled, "I'd have to jump over Dick Gregory. I had the shadow of Gregory in everything I did."

Together, he and Silver tried to find a way out. At the time Cos said, "We decided between us that I didn't have to trade on my being a Negro to succeed. I feel that I have no right to speak for all Negroes any more than a Jewish comedian can speak for all Jews, or, for that matter, any American can speak for all other Americans. . . . I still speak out for equal rights, but I do it as an American, not as an entertainer."

Cos's point of view was simple enough. There was no room for another Dick Gregory. Bill Cosby was a comedian in the Twain mold, observing all aspects of human nature, a comedian who just happened to be black. Dick Gregory's inspiration and cause was that he was a black comedian.

Some nights, Cos would try to stay away from the easy racial one-liners. He would stray into ad-libs, working on long, rambling comic talks on the things he observed riding the subway, the things that happened to him in college. His friend from high school, Ed Weinberger, would occasionally be in the audience, flinching at the mumbling, stumbling words, sharing the pain. Weinberger knew that it was tough creating comedy. He was doing it himself, writing material for Dick Gregory.

Roy Silver would be in the wings watching the trial and error, and error. One lone voice in a dead-quiet room. "He'd listen to the loud absence of laughs for a couple of minutes, panic, and blam!" Cos would spit out a racial gag and save himself. And glare over at Silver, the manager who was encouraging him to slide right down the drain.

Coming offstage in a rage, Cosby would push past Silver, barking out a quick "Up yours!"

The men would shout at each other, fight, and Cos would ball up his fist and shove it at Silver's face, ready to punch some sense into him.

"Next morning, after we'd both cooled off a little, we'd get together and maybe develop another minute or two of material. It would be painful and hard . . ."

Other comedians were finding another way to conquer the audience. Instead of the scattered fire of gags, à la Bob Hope or Henny Youngman, they did minidramas. Jonathan Winters acted out movies. Bob Newhart and Shelley Berman used telephone monologues. Even Joanie Rivers was stringing gags together in long routines about her hairdresser, Mr. Phyllis, and five minutes on buying a wig at a wigpen on a wig farm.

Cos began to build clean, nonracial routines; routines that would be like the Mark Twain stories, so good, so true, so real, you not only laugh when you hear them, but you want to hear them over and over again. They wanted Newhart to do his "driving instructor" bit. They wanted Lenny to do "How to Relax Your Colored Friends," and

Berman had to do "The Morning after the Night Before." What about Cos?

He was developing his football routine into a solid little gem. And he was wringing laughs now from the wave of karate and judo classes in New York, and the way those Jerome Mackey judo parlors were flourishing right next to Vic Tanny. But the bit that really hit was "Noah and the Ark." More than anything else, it established that Bill Cosby was a very funny fellow, in the Mark Twain tradition.

Newspaper articles on the rising young comic began to describe the bit, quoting whole segments of it. Students of comedy, like Steve Allen, would print it almost verbatim, pointing out the gems. But, of course, like most comedy monologues, it had to be heard, as uttered by the comedian, to be fully appreciated.

Cos started it out in the traditional "what if" fashion. He wondered what if Noah were like any skeptical modern cat? And suddenly he heard the voice of God?

"NOAH."

"Who is that?"

"It's the Lord, Noah."

"Right!"

When Noah finally believes he's actually talking to the Lord, he wonders why.

"I want you to build an ark."

"Ri-ight. What's an ark?"

"Get some wood. Build it three hundred cubits by eighty cubits by forty cubits."

"Right. What's a cubit?"

When the Lord tells him he plans to destroy the world, Noah can't believe it: "Am I on *Candid Camera?*"

"I'm gonna make it rain four thousand days and drown them right out!"

"Ri-ight. Listen, do this and you'll save water. Let it rain for forty days and forty nights and wait for the sewers to back up."

"RIGHT!"

Cosby's comedy had a classic feel to it. More than a hundred years before, Mark Twain had produced comic literature hailed as the work of a genius. A look at a Twain biblical satire, "The Diary of Adam and Eve," shows just how close to the heart Cosby had come. Twain's Adam is also a modern skeptic, grumbling about Eve: "This new creature with the long hair is . . . always hanging around, in the way, following me about. . . . I get no chance to name anything myself. The new creature names everything that comes along . . . and always that same pretext is offered: it looks like the thing. There is the dodo, for instance . . . it 'looks like a dodo.' It looks no more like a dodo than I do!"

Twain's Adam grumbles that Eve eats too much, puts up crazy signs like THIS WAY TO THE WHIRLPOOL and THIS WAY TO GOAT ISLAND, and starts coming up with wacky stories like being a part of his rib. "I have not missed any rib," he challenges. But what do you expect from a crazy creature? "She has taken up with a snake now."

Roy Silver recalls the time Danny Kaye came down to the Village, looking for new talent. A showcase was assembled featuring some of Roy's stars, including Cass Elliot and Bill Cosby, and some from another manager, Jack Rollins.

"I don't have to tell you what a major event this was in our lives. Okay? Now Danny came down with an entourage, in a limousine. And Bill was gonna close the show.

"The first act came on, Cass Elliot and the Big Three. Danny saw them, and leaped up and said 'They're on the show!' and we all applauded. Another act came on and he said 'They're on the show!'

"Then Jack Rollins's act came on and Danny said 'He's on the show!' Bill was about to go on, and Danny said 'Well, that's enough . . .' and left. Cosby never got to go on. And he and I in the middle of the street had a screaming argument."

Setbacks like that happened all too frequently. Worse than that were the weeks when there wasn't any work, or anything to look forward to. But, while things were still very sporadic, with several months going by without a significant gig, he *was* getting a few bookings at prestigious clubs, like Chicago's Gate of Horn. He and his manager were still not above riding out and staying in a cheap hotel together—and all for a seventy-five-dollar date—but it was getting better.

"He was in the right place at the right time," Roy Silver recalls. The manager knew that there were people out there who *wanted* to understand and like blacks, especially a guy like Cos who was more likable than a Dick Gregory or Redd Foxx. Best of all, the people were coming in with an open mind. Cosby himself would admit that there was this element in the audience. They hadn't come to see Dick Gregory because they were forced. They wanted to hear him. Cosby could see that there was no chance of convincing anyone of his equality or his humor—if that person wasn't willing to at least meet him halfway in a nightclub.

But there were those long months without big-money gigs. There was the chance that his act wouldn't work outside a few hip big-city clubs. After the summer, Cosby went back to Temple University, confused, tempted by his stand-up success, and restless.

Chapter

6

One weekend Temple had a football game scheduled against an Ohio team. And Cosby had managed to get himself a two-hundred-and-fifty-dollar booking at Town Hall. The coach, George Makris, was worried.

At a meeting with Temple's athletic director, Ernie Casale, George shook his head and said, "You know Cosby, he's involved with this comedy thing. Well, the team's supposed to go out to Toledo on Friday, but he doesn't want to go out.

"He said he can make a couple hundred bucks Friday night being a comedian. He wants to come out Saturday, alone."

"I'll talk to him, George," Casale said.

A short time later, Cos and Casale met. The director looked over Bill's transcripts while the Temple junior waited.

"Bill," Casale said at last, "look at this. You started out, you were an outstanding student, a B student, and now you're in your junior year and your grades are going down. You're trying to do too much. You're participating in track, and football, and you're working nights with all this outside activity . . . you can't do all these things."

"Mr. Casale, do you really mean it would be impossible to do this Friday-night show?"

"Bill," Ernie said apologetically, "I can't permit it. I can't let you go out to Ohio alone, the rules don't allow it. Something might happen to you and all kinds of problems could occur. Besides, they need you first thing Saturday morning."

Ernie Casale can still remember Bill's reaction. Cosby looked up at him and gave him a little smile.

"You know," he told the athletic director, "I think you just made up my mind. I can't pass up that job. I'm gonna turn in my uniform. I'm gonna make it as a comedian."

Recalling it now, Casale adds, "It took a lot of guts to do what he did, but his competitive spirit was such that he thought he could do it."

At the time, one person wasn't sure about it at all: Cosby's mom.

"How could you do it, Bill? How could you!"

The bitter disappointment was painfully evident in her eyes. Cos tried to make her understand. He told her about the gigs. He could get two hundred dollars a week. He'd tried to keep his mind on his studies, but studying the tapes of his comedy shows was more important. The jokes were running through his head. New bits. New routines.

As far as Anna Cosby could see, Bill had ruined his chances for a good career and a good job. And he was so close. If he could just stick it out for another year and a half.

How long had it taken Bill to make it back when he'd dropped out of high school? Four years! How was he ever going to get a second chance and return to college?

Mrs. Cosby was inconsolable. Bill felt the burden of it. Nothing was funny at home. His brother Russell remembers the sense of gloom and disappointment that his mother felt, making it a tense time for everyone. Nothing was funny for Cosby when he went out to the nightclubs. Walking along the cold city streets, he said, "You could get depressed sometimes. Look at the people's faces and you see no happiness, no warmth."

He made the laughter happen in the clubs. The checks kept coming in. Some weeks he still came up short, but the momentum was building as the young comic made the club circuit throughout the Northeast.

He always dreamed about the time when he could say that he'd made the right decision: big time and big bucks.

He got his paycheck one night on the road. He looked at the amount and immediately went back to the club owner, asking to have that week's earnings in cash. In five-dollar bills. Then he went back to his hotel room, grabbed that fistful of money, and flung it in the air, making a blizzard of bucks that came down in swirls of white and green. Four hundred dollars! Bill Cosby: comedian.

It was 1963, the new year, and he was beginning to move. In March he played the Shadows, a club in Georgetown, Washington, D.C., for five hundred dollars a week. Then it was back to the Gaslight for three months to work on new material.

Roy Silver knew a guy in the Warner Bros. publishing division in

New York. He told him about the hot young comedian and told him to get a contract ready. "As a favor," Silver recalls, a Warner vice president, Artie Mogull, began working on the deal. This was another big step for Bill.

Even better, the nightclub crowds were beginning to catch on to his special style of storytelling. Here was something new, audience and comic together as friends, relaxing, sharing warm, truthful, yet hysterically funny experiences.

"Your stuff becomes funny because *you* are delivering it. You're a talking cartoonist, painting images in the audience's head." Cos had told himself that, and now it was true.

Sometimes he still got distracted. Sometimes people still wanted him to do some Dick Gregory bits. They expected it of the black comedian. Cos had to set them straight, politely. "Rather than trying to bring the races together by talking about differences, why not bring them together by talking about all the similarities?"

"I had to be original if I wanted to fulfill my aspirations of becoming a big man in show business," he recalls now. But something was really wrong. People didn't always seem to get the message. He seemed to have to repeat himself. Again. And again. The racial questions came up again and again, making the triumph bittersweet.

Cosby fielded the questions politely, wittily, and tried to concentrate on the importance of getting press coverage and shrug off the dumb questions that went with it.

It was tough sometimes, but it was just as hard to try and piece together steady gigs. Cosby would have to zigzag all over the East Coast just trying to keep the momentum going and the money coming in. Down in Washington, D.C., a friend of his tried to fix him up with a date. He'd heard some nice things about pretty, nineteen-year-old Camille Hanks. But she had heard some pretty awful things about seedy stand-up comics. She refused to see him.

A psychology major at the University of Maryland, Camille enjoyed some of the middle-class lifestyle that was still just a dream for most blacks. The world of her childhood was far different from the environment that spawned the slick comical con artist from Philly.

Camille grew up in the suburb of Silver Springs. There was fresh air and plenty of room. While Cos and his gang had to tinker together go-carts from broken-up wood crates and stolen baby-carriage wheels, Camille could go next door with her friends and ride horses, enjoying rural trails where the ground wasn't littered with broken glass and bottle caps. Cosby's dad cooked in a navy kitchen; Camille's father was a researcher working in the chemistry lab at Walter Reed Hospital.

"Growing up as I did," Camille says, "I believed in everything awful I'd ever heard about show-business people and I was afraid. But later someone brought Bill to my bowling class and he sat in the back, cutting up as usual. He didn't look at all like the ogre I'd expected, so we went out. The second week I knew him he asked me to marry him. Three months later I said yes."

A few moments following that, Camille's parents said no. The engagement was off.

What a rocky road it was for Cos, trying to keep his relationship going with Camille. It was the long, twisty road between New York and Maryland. Working at the Bitter End, in the Village, Cosby would finish up at two or three in the morning. Catching a quick nap, he'd start out for Camille's place at daybreak. Driving down in his used— very used—Dodge seemed to take forever. He'd spend the day with Camille, then drive back in time for the evening's show.

Sometimes when they'd go to the movies, Bill would zonk out, fast asleep.

The more Camille's parents saw of the ardent young suitor, the more impressed they became. Eventually they came around, and the engagement was on again.

The summer of 1963 saw Bill's situation greatly improved in comparison to the previous summer's struggles at the Gaslight. He had perfected his "Noah" routine, had some choice bits on Temple's football squad, stories every New Yorker could identify with about subway nuts turning every car into a sideshow, and even spoofs of commercials. As a dumb jock extolling the wonders of shaving cream, Cos, eyes wide in wonder, talked about how he could take a razor and remove "the little tiny hairs . . . comin' out of my face!"

Cosby was making a name for himself as a rising star, somebody to watch. The trouble was that most of America watched television, and Cosby wasn't getting that exposure. He was barely at the starting gate, earning a couple hundred bucks a week compared to the thousands offered a Jonathan Winters or Shelley Berman.

Bill was developing into an almost irresistible personality. So funny. So nice. But, when it came to auditioning for *The Tonight Show,* the nice guy finished last. The affable smile he put on doing his act would turn into a poisonous frown as he left NBC in defeat.

That summer, Johnny Carson took a week off and hired guest host

Allan Sherman. An overnight sensation, the pudgy, cute comic had been unemployed and near bankruptcy when he scored a fluke hit with a weird album of kosherized comedy songs, *My Son the Folk Singer*. A victim of many professional disasters (his one triumph being the creation of *What's My Line*—which he signed away without even a percentage, hungry as he was for cash up front), Sherman understood what it was like to suffer and wait for a break.

Cosby was playing basketball down on the public court at Waverly and Sixth Avenue, and he barely looked up from the hoops when he got the news. So there's a guest host on *The Tonight Show?* So what.

"Screw 'em," Cos said, sinking another shot that rattled off the wooden backboard and slid through the netless hoop. "They're all fucking assholes. They already turned me down three times and I'm not auditioning for them."

"This is different," his manager said. "This could be it! Give 'em another chance!"

"Yeah," Cos answered, thinking back to the humiliation and rejection, getting excited only to get kicked down. "Why should I put myself through that again?"

Cos shot a few more baskets. Then he stopped.

"All right," he said. "I'll take one more shot at them." When he told reporters that making it in show business took every ounce of guts and determination a guy had, he wasn't kidding.

Cosby raced uptown by cab. There wasn't much time now. He got to NBC at three, and taping was scheduled for five-thirty. Wariness and hostility were written all over Cosby's face as he stormed into the building. But he knew he had to cool it for the audition.

"Hi, Bill," Allan Sherman said. "I'm glad to see you. I've heard so much about you." Cosby nodded, still playing defense. "Why don't you do whatever you would do on the show tonight," Sherman said easily.

Cosby slowly worked himself into the karate bit, making all the gestures and moves in the awkward silence of the guest host's office. He began to get a rhythm going. Sherman wasn't exactly chuckling, but sometimes pros simply appreciate another comic's work without yucking it up.

"Okay, Bill," Sherman said when it was over. "I think that'll be real great. You'll do the show tonight."

Within hours, millions of people all over the country got their first look at Bill Cosby.

Cosby would never forget that night. Twenty years later, discussing it, ironically enough, with Johnny Carson (and no mention was made of who had been hosting *The Tonight Show* at the time), Cos set the scene:

"I came out—the guy put Lena Horne's make-up on me—I walked out and I was going to do my karate routine. And I hadn't really thought that it would be funny. But I guess the people were so conditioned to see a black person come out—they said okay, he's gonna talk about the back of the bus and the front of the restaurant and the side of the tree—and I walked out and I said I wanna talk about karate. And they went *wooo hah hah*—and I almost backed up and said, 'Well, what's so funny?' Then I went into the routine."

He did his impression of a guy who's just graduated from a karate school, proud of "the big slab of callus you got on your hand. It makes your hand look like a foot. Don't laugh. This is good. Keep your hand in your pocket for nine days, then when somebody attacks you, you take a swing at 'em and even if you miss, the smell'll kill 'em."

He showed how to break bricks with the proper histrionic karate shout. And then he told the folks that you could scare robbers without knowing karate—all you needed was the shout. With the crook cringing, you say, "Watch out or I'll shout again. Matter of fact, you give me *your* dough!"

He talked about a karate expert who knew the secrets of the sport: "He says, I'm thinking through this rock, I'm thinking two feet past it. He raised his arm and it came down—unfortunately this rock was thinking, 'No you won't either,' and it shattered his whole elbow . . . now he picks on Jell-O . . . whipped cream . . . we still applaud for him but he's nothing . . ."

Cosby was a hit. In August 1963 he went to Mr. Kelly's in Chicago for five hundred dollars a week and then in September turned up at the Hungry i making seven hundred fifty a week.

In January 1964, the stores had copies of *Bill Cosby Is a Very Funny Fellow . . . Right!*, a live album recorded on Bill's home comic turf, the Bitter End in Greenwich Village.

Allan Sherman produced the record with Roy Silver, and, just as stars as Harpo Marx and Steve Allen had done for Allan's records, Allan filled the back cover with a heartfelt personal endorsement for Bill. Sherman, the top comedy seller of 1962 and 1963, lavished eye-popping praise on Bill Cosby.

Talking about the Noah routine, Sherman wrote that it "is a masterpiece, even though nobody has heard it yet. It's warm, and human, and honest, and deeply moving, and it's funny. It's going to be a classic . . .

if Bill wanted to, he could make a living for the rest of his life just from the excitement and joy this one great bit will create. But Bill Cosby, if I am any judge of talent, will keep coming up with fresh, new material and will grow everyday in stature and importance on the American comedy scene. . . ."

He urged the millions of people who had made his albums gold to pick up on Bill Cosby. "I'm so proud and happy for the chance to introduce you to Bill Cosby," Sherman added. "It isn't every day that we come in contact with greatness."

In 1964, the record racks contained hit albums from many "overnight" sensations. There was the unlikely-looking Barbra Streisand, just another Greenwich Village hopeful a short time ago. And there was the unlikely-looking trio that people said resembled "two rabbis and a hooker," folkies named Peter, Paul, and Mary. And suddenly hitting the charts were the most unlikely-looking people of all, the Beatles.

It was time for something new in comedy. With the push from Allan Sherman, it was time to see a new name on the charts. Bill Cosby, with sales of his new album becoming phenomenal. Sensational.

But they were mediocre. Barely ten thousand copies were sold. And that hardly seemed to suggest that Bill Cosby was a very funny fellow, right?

The important thing was that Cos at least had a record deal. That was a sign of respect, even though Warners only paid $2,500 to sign him up. Another important thing was that his nightclub earnings were getting higher all the time, some weeks topping $1,500. With the club work, and the record now in the stores, there was cause to celebrate.

Best of all, Cosby started off the new year with a new bride. On January 25, 1964, he married Camille in Olney, Maryland. The Warner Bros. comedian and his wife had a whirlwind honeymoon. The newlyweds traveled all over the country. They went to San Francisco—because Bill was appearing at the Hungry i. They went to Los Angeles—because Bill was booked for the Crescendo. Then they went up to Lake Tahoe—where Bill played Harrah's and found himself a favorite of the club's owner, Mr. Harrah himself.

Cosby was part of the new, gentler wave of comedy. Just a few years earlier, stand-up had been dominated by hostile satirists who made their audiences squirm: Sahl, Bruce, Gregory, Berman, Nichols and May. But along with the Kennedy administration had come a youthful enthusiasm, a fresh sense of optimism, and the carefree sense of silliness typified by Allan Sherman's lighthearted parodies. Even satire was gentler, with best-selling albums like *The Button Down Mind of Bob New-hart* and *The First Family.* Audiences were laughing at a pair of baby-faced folkie funsters called the Smothers Brothers. And now there was Bill Cosby.

Or was there? Cos issued a new album, *I Started Out as a Child,* in the fall of 1964, and it sold only nine thousand copies. Warners was ready to drop him from the label.

The momentum was building though. Instead of dying out completely, the first Cosby album was still holding on. Cos was getting more exposure, and the second album solidified his stance as a comedian with a special appeal to the young. It was the first one to touch on such familiar Cosby themes as playing street football, enjoying childhood luxuries like a first pair of sneakers, and the childhood misery of sharing the bed with a younger brother who wet the bed ("Hey—I'm tired of sleepin' on the cold spot!").

Kids were buying comedy records for the first time. They couldn't understand Sahl, but they could love the "Mom Always Liked You Best" of the Smothers Brothers, and they loved Bill Cosby, the man who told them all about his childhood—and theirs. They didn't think of Cos as the Black Comedian. He was just the funniest storyteller they'd ever heard.

Unfortunately, some of the grown-ups weren't as smart.

They couldn't see what he was doing. They kept on asking him why he wasn't doing racial jokes. With Cosby onstage, so equal he didn't have to dignify the bigots by doing gags about his being black, it seemed pretty obvious that Bill was on to something. But backstage, white reporters wanted to hear the Dick Gregory lines, and blacks were suspiciously asking what *else* Cos was doing for the cause.

Cosby began to get the idea that no matter what he did, he wasn't going to be left alone. But he still kept to his image of the patient, laid-back comic, even if his answers starting coming out just a little bit slower, firmer, and with clenched-teeth enunciation.

"It would be easy to get on a stage and talk about 'the Problem,' " he would say. "Now, I have no crutch."

They didn't get it. "But Mr. Cosby, please elaborate."

"*First,*" he began, as though talking to an imbecile, "I'm *tired* of those old jokes about stereotyped Negroes. You *know what I mean?* I don't miss *Amos 'n' Andy. Second,* I'm *tired* of those people who say, 'You should be doing more to help your people.' I'm a comedian, *that's all. Third,* my humor comes from the way I look at things. I am a man.

I see things the way other people do. . . . A white person listens to my act and he laughs and he thinks, 'Yeah, that's the way I see it too.' Okay. He's white. I'm Negro. And we both see things the same way. That must mean that we are *alike. Right?* So I figure this way I'm doing as much for good race relations as the next guy."

Case closed?

Of course not.

The lecture had to be repeated in interview after weary interview.

The lecture also had to be repeated when he was offered television work. "If somebody comes to me and says, 'I want to have you on the show because there's this thing I have about a white guy and . . .' my answer is no. You need a show Negro. Now if you need a comedian, call."

With some TV work, and the nightclubs, Cosby was now a better-known commodity. Not a big star by any means, but able to make a good wage if he kept to the road every week.

People were beginning to remember his name. Bill Crosby. Uh, Bing Cosby. That very funny new comedian Bob Crosby. Bill . . . Cosby?

(Cosby was an unusual name back in 1963, but it's actually quite an old one. Its roots are in the Old English *ceawas-by*, which means "bold ruler's settlement." Now it's certainly doubtful that anyone, even Alex Haley, could trace Bill's relatives to England, but, interestingly enough, the emblem for the Cosby clan features the black leopard. Three of them on a silver background.)

When the Cosby name was so firmly established he could afford some luxuries, Bill splurged. It wasn't simply the allure of knickknacks. There was much more to it than that.

It wasn't the gleam of the gold, it was the gleam in his eye when he could walk into a fancy shop, stand up in front of some snide-looking clerk, plunk down a wad of bills and blow the guy's mind. Gold rings, gold cufflinks, gold tie bars. All those drippingly rich items advertised in the back of *The New Yorker.* Fancy clocks, decorator ice buckets, diamond stickpins. Cos picked them up like he was buying a handful of candy bars.

Cosby's passion, most of all, was cars. Now he was able to get something he could be proud to ride in. He picked up a Mercedes-Benz 300SL.

One night in Los Angeles, Cos happened to meet an old friend from the Village, folk singer Theodore Bikel. When they went out to get their cars and find a place to eat, an interesting contrast was parked in front of them. There was Cosby's Mercedes, immaculate and shiny. And next to it, Bikel's old Corvette, with bumper stickers all over it saying things like WE SHALL OVERCOME.

Bikel looked at his friend's Mercedes, and asked, "What did the Nazis ever do for you?"

Cosby sold the car.

To replace it, he wasn't sure quite what to do. With all the irritations from handling "the Problem" and doing interviews about his "image," he felt guilty about wanting to get a Cadillac. Isn't that the stereotypical car that Negroes love to own? And how can you drive around in a Cadillac anyway if there are poor blacks somewhere without enough change to get a seat in the back of the bus?

It took a long talk with his wife Camille before Bill finally allowed himself the joy of sitting behind the wheel, tooling down the street in his new Cadillac Eldorado.

It took some more long talks with Camille before Bill reluctantly let reporters drive up and visit the Cosby house. He didn't want them in his California home, and he valued his privacy immensely. But he gave interviews because he felt it was important to show the world a young, successful black couple who had achieved "the Dream."

During the interviews, Cos would deflect questions about his childhood and marriage as much as possible. He wanted to let the warm, funny stories of growing up be accepted as fictionalized fact. As for the endless racial questions, he insisted he was just a comic, not a civil rights activist or political leader.

He didn't know that, within months, he would be just what he had long avoided becoming: the center of the rising civil rights movement in America, a reluctant leader who would become one of the key figures in an important moment of black-white confrontation.

Chapter

7

Cos was doing his thing at the Crescendo, a late-night gig for the typical after-dark crowd. There were free spenders, the hipsters, the tipsy chicks hanging on the arms of dates plying them with liquor and laughs.

He did the kind of bits they would respond to. A thing about kissing all night long till your lips got raw. A shot of sick humor in a little vignette where a kid enters a room full of gas, can't see a thing, crawls along the floor, and decides to light a match.

He did his karate bit, drawing waves of laughter with each cockeyed leap, each sudden, manic pose. Imitating a karate expert fending off a mugger in a dark alley, Cos coolly swings around to attack—only to see a midget holding a gun. Oops.

Backstage, Cos met an amiable, balding gent by the name of Carl Reiner. Reiner was impressed with the show. For Bill, who had studied and admired the Reiner and Brooks comedy albums, this was compliment enough. Cos, a stand-up comic for barely two years, was being praised by one of comedy's greatest writers. But Reiner had something else to say. His friend, producer Sheldon Leonard, was also impressed with Cosby, and had seen him do his karate bit on TV. Would Cos care to make an appointment to discuss doing some work with Sheldon?

Cos knew it could only be one thing—a guest spot on *The Dick Van Dyke Show,* which was produced and directed by Leonard and Reiner.

Sheldon Leonard had a tough reputation. For years he'd played gangster parts in movies, and with his olive complexion, dapper short-cropped curly hair, murderous dark eyes so deep and liquid, and jutting lower lip that suggested "stay away," he possessed an intimidating presence. He matched it with a tough personality. Now a TV producer responsible for varied comedy shows like the laid-back, human-interest-oriented *Andy Griffith Show* and another show about real people, the *Van Dyke* series, he was uncompromising in his pursuit of quality. It was Leonard who chose the virtually unknown Van Dyke to star in the latter show, defying network demands for a big star, and reshaping the series after the pilot episode (starring Carl Reiner) was rejected.

Before the riots that would underscore the restless demands for racial equality, Leonard was quietly turning around network concepts on race relations. Reading over an early *Van Dyke* script at the start of the sixties, he was impressed with an episode about Rob Petrie worrying that his newborn baby is not his own. At the hospital, doctors and nurses constantly confused his wife, Mrs. Petrie, with another pregnant woman, Mrs. Peters, who had her baby the same day. But how about this for the capper: Rob discovers that his paranoia is totally misplaced, not because the hospital kept good records after all, but because . . . Mr. and Mrs. Peters are black?

The idea knocked everyone out—everyone except CBS and the show's sponsor, Procter and Gamble. How could Sheldon Leonard even toy with such an idea? And what would the Southern affiliates say? But Leonard stubbornly put his money where his mouth was.

He told CBS he was going to shoot the script anyway, doing it tastefully, using a handsome black couple, Greg Morris and Mimi Dillard. And here was the risky deal: If the live studio audience didn't laugh, if the sequence was offensive, he'd reshoot it with a different ending and different actors, at his own expense.

The half-hour show sped by, with Rob Petrie's comic suspicion growing, till it was time to call up the Peters couple and demand a showdown. When they arrived, and Rob flung the door open, the audience got a good, long look.

It was one of the longest laughs the show ever got, the joke on Rob and his bumbling foolishness. "Why didn't you tell me on the phone?" the embarrassed Petrie asked at last. Greg Morris responded: "And miss the expression on your face?"

To Cosby's shock, Sheldon Leonard didn't want him for an easy, affable comedy spot. He was thinking of Cos to play a role in his new series, *I Spy,* an action-adventure show. A show with an awesome $200,000 budget that would be filmed all over the world. A show that, on the basis of time and money alone, was a tremendous risk for NBC.

Oddly enough, Cos had been perfecting his karate bit well before secret agents like James Bond began thrilling movie audiences with quick neck chops and judo throws. But by 1963, *Dr. No* was a hit at

COSBY . . 51

theaters, President Kennedy was admitting that he had recently read and enjoyed *From Russia with Love,* and television was getting set to welcome *The Man from U.N.C.L.E.,* a show that Ian Fleming had been involved with until he became ill. The character Napoleon Solo was christened by Fleming, after Solo, a character in *Goldfinger.*

In 1964, audiences couldn't get enough. *U.N.C.L.E.* was a hit, and movie spies like James Coburn's Flint and Dean Martin's Helm were ready to compete with Sean Connery. For the fall 1965 season, there would be western spies *(The Wild Wild West)* and comedy spies *(Get Smart)* and something called *I Spy.*

Audiences were ready to accept an American and Russian working together, in the case of *U.N.C.L.E.*'s Napoleon Solo and Ilya Kuryakin. But wait a minute. *I Spy* was starring Robert Culp and who? Negro comedian . . . Bill Cosby? Culp and Cosby? White and black? A thaw in the nation's growing racial cold war?

This was big news all over the country. Newspapers actually headlined the event. And in January 1964, with the pilot episode in the can and NBC still trying to line up sponsors and their stations around the country, insiders were already talking BOMB.

This was going to be the biggest, most expensive bomb in ten seasons, and a tremendous blow to any notion that the American public could accept blacks and whites together. And this was going to brand Negro comedian Bill Cosby as the risk that failed—and, the way show business was, probably drop him face forward into obscurity forever.

In a front-page story, *Variety* headlined, COSBY IN "SPY" PUTS NBC DIXIE AFFILS ON SPOT. They chronicled the tense waiting period and the fate of "television's test case on integration," wondering what the response would be toward a show that "depicts a Negro and a white intermingling on an equal level."

The last time a black co-starred with whites on a TV series had been in the 1950s situation comedy *Beulah.*

For Bill, the waiting period was excruciating on every level possible. But the one he had to deal with, day to day, was trying to make it as an actor. Every day on the set of *I Spy* he had to try, try, and try again to become, overnight, a dramatic actor. All over the country people were likening Cosby to Jackie Robinson. Cos was the "big experiment." But imagine if Jackie Robinson had played football, not baseball, and had been expected to learn every baseball rule in the first season!

Cosby felt guilty. Maybe this part should've been played by a black actor. Maybe somebody like Ivan Dixon, who was toiling away in bit parts on *Perry Mason* and lucky to get them.

The cool, natural comedian was a very uptight actor. At the first reading, when Sheldon Leonard was inspecting the man he had chosen *without* a screen test, Cos was terrible. He knew it himself. He was wooden. He wasn't giving off the excitement and emotion he flashed on a nightclub stage. He was so busy trying to say his lines right that the meaning was wrong. He wasn't paying attention to what the other actors were saying, just tensely waiting for his cue to begin speaking.

Meanwhile, he and Sheldon Leonard were giving interviews of optimism. Cos was under pressure to meet with the press, to endure days when he did nothing but talk, at half-hour intervals, to one glaring reporter after another, and always about the race question. "If [the show] does fail, I hope they won't say we'll never try this again with a Negro. I hope it's a case of Cosby did not come off, not a Negro did not come off.

"Leonard thought it was time that a Negro and a white could play together in a series that did not have any racial overtones," Cos would say, in as stiff a performance as he was giving in rehearsals. "The public," he believed, "will accept my casting."

Sheldon Leonard sounded a little like Branch Rickey. Although he coolly refused to flag-wave for his cause, and tried as best he could to play down the hiring of a Negro, he let slip to a *TV Guide* writer a few words that indicated that, like Branch Rickey, he had made sure that if he was colorblind to talent, he wasn't foolish enough to wreck "the experiment" on someone who didn't have the guts, soul, and stamina to stand up to the tension:

"I was sure he was the man I wanted. I make an intensive underground investigation before choosing a person for a long-range project of this sort. From every source I learned Bill Cosby was a tireless worker, a man striving to do his best. . . ." He added, "Cosby comes on as an engaging, warmhearted, intelligent man. If anyone takes exception to this man because of his color, it will have to be some nut."

Meanwhile, NBC, Leonard, and twenty-seven-year-old Bill Cosby had to wonder what kind of nuts were actually out there. Would any try to storm the studio? Or would there simply be a quiet, efficient boycott? When *The Nat "King" Cole Show* went on the air in the fifties, it was killed in the ratings solely because Southern affiliates refused to carry it, dooming it to a small audience share.

Take a young comic with virtually no acting experience and stick him into a TV show seen by thirty million people. That alone has driven actors over the edge. Now take a man used to intimate nightclubs buzzing with live, appreciative people, and put him on a deathly quiet soundstage at seven in the morning. And instead of ad-libs and surefire jokes, give him scripted dialogue and long, dull stretches of time between every take for him to think, think, and think about it all.

And just for extra fun, make him black, the center of the TV season's greatest controversy.

"Ten years from now," Cos said, "nobody would probably notice that a TV star is Negro or white. At this point, we hope the story is all that matters."

The story *was* the story. What made *I Spy* stand out from the start was the concept behind the show. Even in its embryonic treatments, the idea was to show a spy duo different from Napoleon Solo and Ilya Kuryakin—guys who saved each other's lives but didn't share each other's lives.

I Spy was the story of Kelly Robinson (Robert Culp), a spy traveling the globe as a tennis player, and Alexander Scott (Cosby), spy and Rhodes scholar, undercover as Kelly's trainer-advisor. And it was the story of two men who were comrades, who enjoyed each other's company. In real life, Cos and Bobby *did* enjoy each other's company.

Robert Culp didn't share Cosby's experience of ghetto childhood, but he did share many of Bill's ideals and interests. Professionally he had the same drive toward creativity and quality. Six years older than Cos, Culp had been a youthful loner, an outsider whose edge in school was athletics. He was a champ on the track field, a pole-vaulter with Olympic possibilities. Like Cos, Bobby was sidetracked in college and developed an interest in show business. He starred in a series, *Trackdown,* but got the reputation for being moody and difficult because he refused other shows, determined to hold out for better acting assignments. He also wanted to develop himself as a writer and director, things actors at the time were not supposed to do, or know how to do.

Sam Peckinpah, who directed a few *I Spy* episodes, assessed Culp as a man: "Bob is incensed by prejudice. He doesn't recognize it. He doesn't understand it. Yet he is not trying to carry any particular banner on the show."

Cos and Culp developed a style for the show. The idea was to show a hip, "beautiful" relationship. "My people would just like to enjoy an hour of TV where a Negro isn't a problem," Cosby said. "People can see I'm a Negro; we don't need to say anything else." Culp added, "We're two guys who don't know the difference between a colored and a white man. That's doing more than a hundred marches. We're showing what it could be like if there had been no hate."

On the set, Culp loosened Cos up, and helped him when it would've been easy to upstage him and drive him from co-star status to sidekick.

"Bob gives me the help I need," he told writer Robert de Roos. "As an insecure entertainer coming in to work as an actor, I need all the acceptance I can get—not just hand-shaking, but real acceptance. Bobby gives me that."

Culp answered: "He is the fastest natural study I've ever seen. He is cramming ten years of education into a few months. No novice, no matter how talented, can come up with performances like Bill . . . to become another guy and have another guy's emotions with a bit of hero juice thrown in—that is painfully hard to learn."

It was stinging to have to be directed around the soundstage, to blow a scene because he was facing the wrong way, or not following the marks on the floor, or listening to the foreign language of technical terms shouted by the crew. The "natural" had to learn unnatural, staged choreography, and make it look natural again.

"They move you around from seven in the morning to seven at night as though you were an index card," he said. "I am still tumbling around the fringes of performances—playing with the outside edge. I've been trying to do the story lines without camping—to get a laugh as an actor, not as a comedian, and it's not easy. Everybody tells me I'm too self-critical. Well, we'll see."

Some around the set figured that maybe it wasn't just faith in himself, but perhaps some kind of religious comfort that was helping to pull him through. But Cos was never very religious. "I'm sort of a frightened atheist. If the sky were to open up tomorrow, I'd cop out. I'd probably try to con God. There are a few things I'd like to say to Him . . . but I don't think it can be done by prayer."

Anxiety was high not only at NBC, but at agencies like William Morris. Executives there screened an early episode of *I Spy,* and they were aghast. How could sponsors be talked into advertising on this show? How could affiliates be persuaded to take it? Just look at what was going on!

There was a scene where Bill was on a bridge, making a contact with a pretty young girl. It was a long shot. All he really had to do was stay there for a moment, make the connection, and that was it. He kissed her cheek and walked off.

"You'll never get this on the air," one of the Morris men said. "Good God, he's kissed a white girl!"

Actually, Bill had done nothing more than kiss his wife Camille. They'd needed an extra for the short scene, and they called the first lady they happened to see hanging around the set.

With each new episode, Cos began to deliver his lines with greater confidence, using a whole range of subtle facial gestures and physical stances. As it turned out, as an actor he didn't have to worry about criticism. As he admitted with cautious optimism to those on the set, he had found his rhythm. By the seventh or eighth episode, the balance was struck between the tough, Rhodes scholar–CIA man Scott and cool, easygoing comedian Cos. The result was a sly spy, with a little dash of wry.

As more and more shows were completed and the date for the *I Spy* premiere crept closer, the affiliated stations around the country began to make their decisions. Since they were only affiliates, they were under no obligation to take *every* show the NBC network put on the air. They could grab something from CBS or ABC, produce their own show, or even fill the spot with reruns. CBS had not yet withdrawn the old *Amos 'n' Andy* show from syndication. Even that was possible.

Cos got the word at last. The returns were in: To the surprise of many in the business, the affiliates had overwhelmingly supported the show. They wanted to see Bill Cosby in action with Robert Culp. Only four stations declined the show—stations located in Savannah, Georgia; Albany, Georgia; Daytona Beach, Florida; and Birmingham, Alabama.

Bill Cosby didn't have to feel self-critical now.

Besides, as *I Spy* hit the air across the nation, there were plenty of people, black and white, to do all the criticizing.

Chapter

8

"At 28, Cosby has accomplished in one year what scores of Negro actors and comedians have tried to do all their lives," *Newsweek* wrote. "He has completely refurbished the television image of the Negro. He is not the stereotyped, white-toothed Negro boy with a sense of good rhythm. He is a human being, and a funnier, hipper human being than anyone around him."

When the first shows hit the air, the *New York Herald Tribune* assessed him as an actor: "Mr. Cosby may never get to play more than himself, but since he's an ingratiating fellow, he'll do fine. Gary Cooper went farther on less."

So that was a relief. And as for *I Spy*'s competition, the show was matching CBS's variety series starring Danny Kaye, and destroying the hastily rescripted *Amos Burke, Secret Agent,* which had been about a flamboyant millionaire cop (Gene Barry) the year before, and was now attempting to be trendy.

Predicted to run dead last, *I Spy* was in the Top 20. And a man with virtually no acting experience except for his role in a fifth-grade production of *King Koko from Kookoo Island* ended the year winning an Emmy Award as best dramatic actor in a series. Yet there was no time when Cos could fully lift his head up and enjoy the triumph.

"I've been watching my step all the way," he sighed. "I never wanted to be judged as temperamental or nasty. If you're snotty then people would be sure to say, 'Those Negroes are all alike . . . I don't want them biting me!'

"The show is exhilarating in some ways and a burden in others. The character I play is a highly educated man and I'm nowhere near that. I was never a great student . . . and he is a Negro 'good guy' working equally with a white man for a patriotic cause—a premise which may not be accepted by every Negro watching."

And how could he pretend to support the CIA, and how could he do shows without inserting a few words on the growing civil rights movement, and why wasn't there a scene where Scotty is forbidden from coming into the same hotel as Kelly, and on and on and on.

And Cosby found himself defending, in interview after interview, against the innuendo that simply being Bill Cosby was not good enough. That his accomplishments toward equality were not good enough. That his milestone achievement in breaking into TV was not good enough.

"Bill Cosby carries as much weight on his shoulders as any Negro I know, and he wears it as well and as lightly as any man could. He may not be a front-runner in the cause—that's not his nature—but he's totally committed. He gives freely of his time and money. In Watts, he's worked hard for community theater. The cats on the street corner dig him, and he represents something very important to me."

Sammy Davis, Jr., said that. But then, many blacks and whites attacked him, too, for the very same reasons.

Those who wanted to could find a subtle message on how Cos felt by taking a look at the cartoon he clipped from a magazine and put on his dressing room wall. It showed a smiling prisoner in chains, up against a cobblestone wall, facing the hooded torturer who stood before him carrying a whip. "Well," the prisoner says to the torturer, "are we feeling any better today?"

Fortunately, Cos got to put the questions behind him and go out on location, shooting exteriors in exotic parts of the world. Sheldon Leonard reasoned that part of the allure of the international spy world was in the international locales. Instead of resorting to fakery, he insisted on bringing his actors to Hong Kong, Italy, and Spain to capture the distinct flavor of each country. It was in Hong Kong that Bill received news that his first child, Erika Ranee, was born, on April 8, 1965. It was also in Hong Kong that the Cosby cool was tested by a variety of natural and man-made problems.

On some days Hong Kong resembled a war zone, with storming typhoons whipping trees and debris through the air at a hundred miles per hour. The citizens fled the streets, even those used to the eye-popping winds that brought with them torrential downpours of sizzling rain.

Shooting sequences on the crowded streets of Hong Kong was often as chaotic as a typhoon. Cos and the crew would set up for a day's work, threatened by gray skies and mottled clouds above, with the teeming, curious citizenry swarming around on all sides. Simple scenes had to be done again and again as translators shouted instructions to the extras and snarled traffic was rerouted to flow more naturally. As it was, it was almost impossible for the roving cameras and walking actors to wend their way through the crowds without stepping over somebody or knocking into someone.

Sometimes a day's shooting captured the purple-blue waters of the bay, and the richness of the green and brown mountains, a tantalizing feast for lucky viewers at home who were just buying their first color TV sets, finding out what the NBC peacock really looked like. But just as often the out-takes would show tragicomic scenes of bewildered Orientals careening into the scenery and arguing with each other in voices of anger and woeful dismay.

Even though the camera crew took to hiding the cameras in boxes, and camouflaging them behind trees, there would be scenes of Cosby and Culp talking—obliterated by the huge, blinking face of an amazed Hong Kong citizen staring into the magic glass.

Cos and his manager had to keep a watchful eye on the script. In one lighthearted sequence, a curious Oriental child was supposed to be captivated by Cos, and then coyly rub his face. The child was supposed to say, "Oh. Brown no come off?" The only thing that came off was that scene in the script.

Gradually the scripts began to include more and more of the low-key Cosby humor. Cosby's tongue-in-cheek comedy was perfect to liven up the cloak-and-dagger drama. In one sequence, he and Culp are confronted and outnumbered by the bad guys:

"Let's rush 'em," Cosby whispers.

"I'll be right behind you," says Culp.

"That's no good. When we have to run away you'll be in front of me."

In another episode, Cosby is about to dive into the swimming pool (true to his spy nature, he's wearing sunglasses, in addition to the scuba mask up on his forehead). He's stopped by Culp, who has noticed that the pool is wired with electricity.

Shrugging off the narrow escape, Cos recalls another villain who used to like to shock people: "His name was Feeney. He was real trouble in school. He'd wire himself up, shake hands, and buzz ya. *Thipp!* He was the only guy the principal gave a diploma to with rubber gloves on."

Cosby's comedy and delivery were so infectious, Robert Culp began to pick up on it. After starting out as a "straight" hero, Bobby began using Cosby catch-phrases, offering a hip "Oh, isn't that wonderful" in the face of danger, or asking, "Is that a fact?" and "Does that shake your tree?" Culp ended up spouting some pretty Bill-ious lines, like: "If you don't get out of here very shortly, to enjoy the scenic wonders of this lovely land, the dwarfs are gonna come out and pull your beard down to your kneecaps!"

NBC was a little alarmed by all that, but it was certainly proof that a black guy and a white guy could communicate with each other. Offstage, Cos could say "Bobby knows me better than anybody does. We're closer than brothers and we are equal in the show and out of it."

They were a matched pair when it came to causing trouble, too. In one scene they were supposed to rush up to a twenty-foot-high wall and pretend to climb it. Then the stunt men would take over, do the actual climbing, race over the rooftop, and then jump down into a convenient alleyway.

Well, the veteran track stars had other ideas. When they reached the wall, whispering suspiciously to each other, giggling with impromptu laughter, they not only took hold of the wall, but started climbing. The two athletes matched each other stride for slippery stride, making it up the wall with amazing ease. The awed crew watched as Bobby and Cos ran across the roof like real spies, skittered down slanted rooftops, and finally made their leap into the alley.

They'd done it! Only the crew had been so surprised, not a second of it was caught on film.

Sheldon Leonard usually caught the heavy mistakes. There was the time two stunt men were called upon to take a dive into the sea. But Sheldon found out the two men couldn't swim. He found it out "after they had followed my instructions and jumped into Hong Kong harbor . . ."

Once the cry went out for a fish, a big, beautiful sailfish crucial to a particular harbor scene. It took a long time for one of the fishermen to catch a suitable subject. But when shooting had to be rescheduled for the following day, the fish was carefully tied up and hooked to the side of the dock, kept fresh in the cool water. The next morning it was hauled up, nothing but a prickly skeleton. During the night it had been picked to pieces by scavenging harbor fish.

Writer Dick Hobson recalled the time Cosby ran up against Chinese superstition: "In Hong Kong the script called for him to be shot down, suddenly revive and shoot the pursuing 'heavy' dead. Unhappily Cosby had to fall with his face next to a pigsty. Which made him doubly anxious to do the scene in one take. But the Chinese heavy wouldn't die a convincing death. On the first take he died with one leg sticking up in the air; on the second he kept whirling around and wouldn't fall dead; on the third he 'died' in a sitting position. It took five takes for them to realize he thought cameras capture the soul. He was not about to simulate real death for fear it would come true." Meanwhile Cos had to keep dying with him, falling down and hoping that, for a change, his nemesis would also bite the dust and stay there.

Cosby's spirits were boosted by reports from stateside of the show's solid ratings. But the real lift came when Erika was, at four months, old enough to travel. She flew to Japan along with Camille and Bill's mom.

While the image of the *I Spy* duo was of two carefree spies enjoying the exotic locations and exotic women, and living the carefree bachelor life, the reality was far different for Cosby. And he loved that reality.

Wherever he went, he took his family, giving his mom a nonstop vacation, the chance to see the world in luxury and triumph. Meanwhile, the triumph included miles and miles of stockings in the hotel bathroom, tons and tons of suitcases for the ladies' clothes, and barely a grip or two for Cos. But it was all worth it. Even waking up extra early —when toddling Erika would come over, giggle, and slug him awake with a fist in the face.

The globe-trotting adventure included stops in Spain, Venice, and Mexico. Back home, Cos capped another season with another Emmy Award.

Cosby enjoyed coming back home to spend more time with his family. "As a father," Camille said, "he's a very gentle man. He's just crazy about the baby and so patient. He loves to bathe her and feed her and dress her. He's just a very loving father. As a husband, he has the same qualities."

In the summer of 1966, another baby was on the way. Cosby was getting in some nightclub work, but hoping that this time he'd be around to see his child be born.

On Saturday, Camille went into the hospital early in the evening. Cos wanted to stay, but he had a date to play. He called the airport and chartered a plane, delaying as long as he could.

He arrived barely in time for the show in Denver; a police escort with sirens blaring drove him to the concert. Cos did his full show, then zoomed back to the airport with another police escort. He raced back to the hospital, arriving around two A.M. Sunday morning.

This child was certainly like her father: she waited until everybody was present, not showing herself until the wee hours of the morning.

Cos was thrilled to actually see the birth of Erinne Chalene Cosby. But pretty soon it was time to get back in harness for the new season of *I Spy.*

It had happened on *The Man from U.N.C.L.E.,* where the conventionally handsome Robert Vaughn was eclipsed by the freak popularity of blond, Beatle-haircut-wearing David McCallum. Now another somewhat blandly handsome performer, Robert Culp, was in the backseat while amiable, funny Cos won the awards. Cos was well aware of the situation. When he won his first Emmy he said in his acceptance speech, "I extend my hand to a man by the name of Robert Culp. He lost this because he helped me."

It *was* supposed to be slanted the other way—like Robert Vaughn the star meant to overshadow sidekick McCallum, like Robert Conrad, on the spy show *The Wild Wild West,* who got the girls while Ross Martin amused them with his makeup wizardry. Robert Culp was supposed to be the main star, with cool, funny support from his partner Bill.

After all, the show was called *I Spy,* not *We Spy,* and in the opening credits, only one silhouette—Culp's—was shown playing tennis, smashing overhand strokes, and then trading racket for gun and shooting up villains. But it was obvious that without Cosby, or some other very unique partner, the *I Spy* hour would be a long, slow one.

Culp could be as moody as Cos, fighting his own battles for professional respect. But the friendship between Cosby and Culp was strong enough to survive the very real, very tense time when the Emmys always went to Cosby and the reporters went to Culp to ask why.

Culp handled the questions tersely, abruptly, not wanting to get into a prolonged debate about the situation, not wanting to slip and lose his cool, blowing up his own disappointment while Cos was in the spotlight.

The spotlight on Cos was casting some glare, too. With every article on the success of *I Spy* came parenthetical questions. Yes, that Cosby is quite a fellow, but the show *is* spy fantasy and does not accurately mirror the average black man's experience in America. Yes, it's certainly wonderful that a black man is on TV, but couldn't he be a little more militant? And how come Scotty never seemed to get involved with women?

For Cos, the whole thing was crazy.

One day he noticed the word *crazy* had been deleted from one of the *I Spy* scripts. The censors had taken it out. He discovered that it was a taboo word. You weren't allowed to use *crazy* in the dialogue because another adventure show had done that—and NBC had received too many complaints from crazy people.

Happily, Cos was part of this great advance for crazy people. But behind the scenes, he was doing everything he could to make his role prideful and relevant to the black community.

With each year, slowly, Cos was trying to do as much as he could. At first there was no love interest for Alexander Scott because it was felt that the image of the "sex-crazed Negro" needed to be remedied. Scott was going to be a hero, not the kind of infantile macho fantasy that James Bond was, with the sniggering sex jokes and obsession with bedding and forgetting his conquests. When the time was right, Scott did get a share of the ladies. And for the first time, young black actresses had more to do than play the part of personable maids or demure secretaries. Cos, who had deliberately wanted his character "sterile," was now deliberately requesting some romance in the scripts.

This still wasn't enough for some. Why, in the midst of the riots and the turmoil and the fight for equality, wasn't Cosby going to bed with *white* women?

In answer to a London *Times* article headlined WHY COSBY NEVER GETS A WHITE GIRL, he patiently told a writer, "Now don't get it wrong. It was my decision right from the start to play it that way. As long as I'm on the screen, whether television or films, I will never hold or kiss a white woman. Hey, our black women have just nothing to look forward to in films, nothing to identify with . . . tell me, how often do you see a black man falling in love and making love with a black woman? So as it is, I want to be seen only with our women—not Chinese or Filipino women, not yellow, green, pink, or white. Just our women, black ones."

With the concept of "black is beautiful" still just a concept, Cos's ideal was inviolate. He was determined to show the beauty of black women. "The black person has been taught for years that he's ugly and she's ugly. The time comes when you say, 'Heck, I'm not ugly, blackness is not ugliness.' "

His people had to learn it too, back in the late sixties. "In cities like

Washington, D.C., in fact," Cos told *Playboy,* "there are many Negroes who still feel a great deal of resentment if a dark Negro comes to date a light-skinned girl. The parents of that girl want to keep breeding lighter, so they can finally get rid of that badge and walk free. But most black people have finally discovered they've been deluding themselves."

Reporters continued to play up the racial question, sometimes goading Cosby, hoping to provoke an explosive controversy (like I SPY STAR SLUGS NOSY NEWSPAPERMAN maybe). Asked about attending the non-violent marches down South, Cos said, "I don't want to go someplace where they're throwing rocks unless I have some rocks to throw back." He continued to resist the urge to throw a few punches at the reporters, preserving the dignity and image he had fought to bring to the character of Alexander Scott.

The year *I Spy* began, the Writers' Guild set up a "Negro Writers' Workshop." Now that *I Spy* was a hit, more opportunities came for black writers, technicians, and actors. Over on *The Dick Van Dyke Show* Sheldon Leonard now hired Godfrey Cambridge to play Harry Bond, secret agent, in an episode called "The Man from My Uncle." It helped secure Godfrey roles in adventure movies in years to come. And following the Cosby lead, Greg Morris (the unknown who played Mr. Peters in the fateful interracial *Van Dyke* episode) was co-starring on *Mission Impossible*—and he was playing the brainy electronics wizard, while white Peter Lupus was the hulking strongman.

The Culp and Cosby duo paved the way for shows that did choose to experiment with white and black themes. Only after a show like *I Spy* could there have been *The Outcasts,* where Otis Young played a former slave and Don Murray a bigoted cowboy. They had lines that could never have been spoken by Alexander Scott and Kelly Robinson:

"With you or without you, I'm going down there tonight in the dark."

"Well, you do have a natural advantage in the dark, don't you, boy. Unless of course you smile."

The Outcasts were billed as "friendly enemies" but *The New York Times* missed the "Robert Culp–Bill Cosby camaraderie of *I Spy*" and saw that particular show as nothing special, except for "the novelty of seeing racial hostility made explicit in a television program."

After three seasons, the spy craze had lost its steam. Dozens of secret agents had flooded the air: new comedy agents (Red Buttons), British agents *(The Avengers* and *Secret Agent),* spin-offs *(The Girl from U.N.C.L.E.),* and spin-outs *(T.H.E. Cat* with Robert Loggia and *Blue*

Light with Robert Goulet). Even the show that had started it all, *The Man from U.N.C.L.E.*, was limping to the end of its run. Shifted to Monday nights opposite *The Carol Burnett Show* and *Big Valley*, *I Spy*'s ratings just deteriorated further. It was game, set, and match after three years.

Cos had mixed emotions. He was relieved that this ground-breaking grind was over. And he had to admit that, because of the exhausting schedule, some episodes of the show had emerged as little more than travelogues with some mystery thrown in. But at the same time, he felt that with another season he might've been able to add even more depth to the character of Alexander Scott, especially since Culp had begun to assume more of the writing and directing duties.

Young fans could still play Kelly and Scott on the home board game of *I Spy*, and everyone could take in the reruns. The show is still seen in syndication today—and its popularity has received a boost from the success of *The Cosby Show*. While the show seems dated, as any sixties spy show must, Bill's unique contribution is still clearly visible. He succeeded at presenting a positive image of equality where none had been before. As he told *Playboy*, he made Scott human, he made him like himself, "a guy who grew up in the ghetto, who went to school and took on middle-class values, who was trying to live like the white middle-class. But he always knew he was black, with a real degree of black pride. . . ."

Cos had won three Emmy Awards in a row. Now what? He'd been talking about retirement, going back to school. Others thought he should star in his own show. And there was his stand-up comedy, netting him Grammy Awards every year.

"You mean," people asked Cos, "there's actually a *decision* to make between making a million bucks a year or going back to school?"

Cos wanted school. And he wanted to continue the momentum of his career. There was no compromise in Bill Cosby. So he vowed to defy them all and do both.

Chapter
9

Nineteen sixty-seven had been a great year for Cos; the Internal Revenue Service told him so. They wanted their share: $833,000 in income tax.

He tried to outrace them in January 1968. With shooting virtually complete on *I Spy*, he did a month of one-night stand-up gigs—25 in all. The take was $750,000 for the month.

The tour reaffirmed in bold figures that, even if *I Spy* was fading away, Bill's popularity was as strong as ever. He was still the nation's hottest comic.

He had no shortage of material. Not only was he able to put together solid, twenty-minute routines about his brother Russell, he was now telling audiences about his new family, his daughters Erika and Erinne. Rather than talk about his childhood, he could talk about theirs. It was comedy through observation instead of filtered through memory, but the laughs came out just the same.

Bill wasn't doing a routine when he talked about his daughters to cooking columnist Johna Blinn. Johna wanted his personal recipe for Scrapple meatloaf, but Cos sidetracked her. "Did you ever watch a one-year-old eat?" he asked. "They never put the food in their mouths but stuff the string beans or peas into their ears or noses. Any cool cook knows that the mashed potatoes have to be just the right temperature before they can be mashed into the hair. . . .

"No kid that age drinks her milk; she just spills it down the front. And then there's always the dropping game, but you can beat that. You have only to fasten a rubber band on the cup handle and wrap it around the child's wrist. That way the kid digs the rubber band and has all the fun of dropping the cup."

Cosby's $215,000 California home was a happy one, with his wife, his two daughters, and his mom. The house had a game room, complete with pool table and card table. And if that wasn't exciting enough, you could always watch the fish tank: There, a pair of piranha showed how to make goldfish disappear.

The household expanded with the arrival of three dogs—Boogie, Sab, and Fat Albert—who somehow managed to keep away from the fish tank and the swimming pool. To keep his weight down, Cos favored a swimming-and-sauna regime, though he also liked participating in "Hollywood All-Stars" basketball games with friends like Bill Russell and Lew Alcindor, who would later change his name to Kareem Abdul-Jabbar.

To get away from it all, Cosby enjoyed long drives. His favorite new "toy" was his hot new Shelby, replacing in his affections the Mercedes, the Cadillac, and the Ferrari, and even the 1937 Rolls-Royce. Sometimes he would drive into the deserted flatlands and gun the motor, racing it almost up to its two-hundred-mile-per-hour capabilities. He loved the car so much he began to talk about it in his act, eventually putting together a twenty-minute routine on sports-car driving, complete with rumbling, purring sound effects.

These days he could even insert a little timely racial humor. He imagined a sports car so dangerous that just stepping on the gas could propel someone down the block and into a tree. That car he'd give away —to George Wallace.

Cos was more and more interested in free-form comedy, meeting the audience face-to-face. "I feel that in-person contact with people is the most important thing in comedy. While I'm up onstage, I can actually put myself into the audience, and adjust my pace and timing to them. I can get into their heads through their ears and through their eyes. Only through this total communication can I really achieve what I'm trying to do."

He was also serious about keeping it a "family show." "It's a conscious effort on my part to stay away from anything that has to do with sex or what are known as four-letter words, unless it is to make a point. Not that I think it's bad; it's just that I'd rather work without using it."

He was staying away from traditional smoky nightclubs, preferring more family-oriented accommodations. "I like to see my people comfortable, not crammed into a small club and paying a hefty cover charge. I have nothing against the nightclub business, but places like Madison Square Garden and the Westbury Music Fair are better. Westbury even more so, because the parking is better and the people

When the press came to his door, the newly signed star of *I Spy* had to keep smiling. He was the "Jackie Robinson of TV," and one false move, one show of temper could have blown it for his career and for all blacks on TV. *(Courtesy Sylvia Norris/Photo Trends)*

The rising young comic was, according to costar Bob Culp, "the angriest person I ever encountered." Cos resented the pressure of his role as a "black symbol," and was tense about switching from comedy to dramatic acting—in front of twenty million people. *(Courtesy Ron Galella)*

A quiet moment for Cosby. The *I Spy* series, his emergence as an Emmy- and Grammy-winning superstar, and his marriage all occurred within a few tumultuous years. *(Courtesy Sylvia Norris/Photo Trends)*

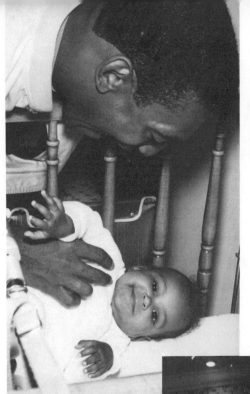

"As a father," Camille said, "he's a very gentle man. He's just crazy about the baby and so patient . . . a very loving father. As a husband, he has the same qualities." *(Courtesy Sylvia Norris/Photo Trends)*

The rare public side of Camille Cosby. On February 17, 1968, she modeled at a "Mom 'n' Moppets" Fashion Show at the Beverly Hilton Hotel with daughters Erinne (left) and Erica (right). *(Courtesy Joe Shere/Pictorial)*

Spy on the run: Cos was fiercely determined to achieve financial stability for his family. On a break from *I Spy* Cos toured the country, performing twenty-five times in thirty days, grossing $750,000. *(Courtesy Ron Galella)*

Culp, Cos and their ladies go out on the town. The *I Spy* show could have been a disaster except for the unexpected: When the two stars met, they formed an enduring, supportive friendship. *(Courtesy Sylvia Norris/Photo Trends)*

"Take my tonsils out? They put you in this hospital gown with no back! You back away from people, right into the cold marble wall!" Cos shares this classic hospital trauma on his first TV special, March 18, 1968. *(Courtesy Pictorial Parade)*

"Baby, everything is all right. Uptight, outta sight!" Cos sang on his first TV special, when he dared to do a show without guest stars—something unheard of at the time. He also out-maneuvered network executives, who tried to shelve the show. *(Courtesy Pictorial Parade)*

A serious Cosby behind the scenes. In 1969 he was the center of a bizarre controversy: a *Tonight Show* appearance TV critics declared an anti-Catholic "blasphemy that won't soon be forgotten." *(Courtesy Ron Galella)*

Let the Harlem Globetrotters clown: Cos is *serious!* He's charging toward a two-pointer in this charity game between the Globetrotters and "The Hollywood Celebrities" on January 25, 1969. *(Courtesy Frank Edwards/Fotos International)*

Above left: "He can pull off nearly anything," *The Christian Science Monitor* wrote when Bill played Aesop in an "Aesop's Fables" TV special in 1971. But Bill's commitment to "family" viewing led to two unsuccessful series in 1972 and 1976, and near video oblivion. *(Courtesy Movie Still Archives)*

Above right: In a courageous early attempt to bring dignity to "blaxploitation" films, Cos sank more than a quarter of a million dollars of his own money into *Man and Boy,* when execs at major studios refused to produce it. One told him, "But there were no black cowboys in the early West." *(Courtesy Movie Still Archives)*

Below right and facing page, top: The *I Spy* duo of Cosby and Culp takes a stand in 1972's *Hickey and Boggs.* Culp said it was about "two super losers trying to pull it out one last time." At the box office, it lost. *(Courtesy Movie Still Archives)*

The outrageously hirsute William H. Cosby, Jr., ready to punch his way out of a hairy moment with Sidney Poitier in *Uptown Saturday Night*. *(Courtesy Movie Still Archives)*

Cosby and Poitier cooked up the right formula, so they said *Let's Do It Again*, in the second of their three films together. *(Courtesy Movie Still Archives)*

Above left: A real basketball enthusiast, Cos is friendly with many basketball stars, from Bill Russell to Dr. J. In 1976 he bought a share of the Philadelphia Warriors, just for the fun of it. *(Courtesy Frank Edwards/Fotos International)*

Above right: Cosby was the teacher, the critics were the slow learners. They criticized *The Bill Cosby Show* for its "slice of life" episodes that were low on sitcom one-liners. It proved to be the only hit of the 1969 TV season. *(Courtesy Movie Still Archives)*

Left: Cosby as Chet Kincaid teaches a carpenter (played by Joaquin Martinez) all he needs to know to pass his citizenship test in a typical "episode with a message." *(Courtesy Movie Still Archives)*

don't have to drive into the city. Plus, they're not drinking and there's no extra tab laid on them."

Sometimes Cos stayed out of nightclubs for other reasons. One day his agent asked him if he'd mind coming to his son's bar mitzvah. Cos agreed. But a short time later, the agent received a booking request from a nightclub: $25,000 for the weekend. The same weekend as the bar mitzvah. The agent was all set to accept the $25,000 date, but Cosby refused. The bar mitzvah was more important.

Something else was becoming important to Cos: his singing career. Although he insisted he was just an "amateur" having fun, he began to book himself into places like the Whiskey-à-Go-Go for "music only" shows, starting in the summer of 1967. Nightclub audiences used to Bill Cosby, comedian, now saw "Silver Throat": Bill Cosby, R&B vocalist.

Was he for real? At first nobody could be sure. Now he was sporting a huge walrus mustache, and that certainly didn't look real. When fans picked up the *Silver Throat Sings* and *Hooray for the Salvation Army Band* albums, they heard some tracks that sounded a little funny—but who knew if that was always intentional?

Many cuts were satirical, like Cosby's exaggerated shout-singing rave-up of "Sgt. Pepper's Lonely Hearts Club Band." But others were definitely sincere, like "Sunny," where Cosby's thin baritone attempted to solemnly croon some life into lines like "I want to thank you, girl, for the wonderful time I had."

The most successful cuts were the ones where he comically strained his voice and scuffed his way through R&B classics. For something like Sam & Dave's "Hold On! I'm Comin'," he knocked out the old lyrics and ad-libbed his own frantic words of encouragement: "You better hold on," he wails to his love. "Try and do something . . . run around the room a lot . . . I might be out of breath, but I'm coming!"

Cos was feeling a little less restricted about putting a little funk into his act, and he educated the more middle-class members of his fan club in the basics of R&B, courtesy of his back-up group, the Watts 103rd Street Rhythm Band.

Those who considered Cosby's foray into vocalizing just egotistic, hard-headed indulgence had to eat their words when Cos punted one of his songs, "Little Ole Man," onto the charts for a while. Some thought the idea of a comedian being musical was funny in itself, but actually the great majority of comics *are* musical. There's a link between monologue rhythms and music. An entire band could be assembled of stand-up comics alone: Henny Youngman (violin), Pete Barbutti (accordion),

Jackie Vernon (trumpet), Johnny Carson (drums), Woody Allen (clarinet), Phyllis Diller (piano)—not to mention Shelley Berman on Jew's harp and Jean Shepherd thumping his head.

By the time the novelty of Cosby's singing career had worn off late in 1968, he was already involved in plenty of other projects. He was hoping to fulfill his ambition of returning to school, and it seemed like the best bet was at the University of Massachusetts. He was even telling interviewers he was going to retire and become a schoolteacher. But he couldn't walk away from show business, especially since it seemed that no matter how much money he earned, taxes took out a huge bite, and bewildering investment options had to be taken into account to ensure that he would not be "embarrassed" by finding himself suddenly broke.

When you talk about show business, he told an *Ebony* interviewer, don't leave off the word *"business.* It's a serious, *serious* business. Most of us come from a low economic background where money is used to just pay bills. We are stunned when we realize that we can make a lot of money. We have no idea how the system works that is going to pay us so much money, so we leave off the most important part—protecting that money."

Now part of a growing corporation, Campbell/Silver/Cosby, he was working on investment deals that could net him a couple of hundred thousand dollars a year for life, even if he never worked again. Creatively, he had his $40,000-a-week stand-up gigs at Harrah's and other clubs, and had negotiated a sweet deal with NBC that would net him a new TV show, his own variety specials, and a few cartoon specials based on Cosby's childhood characters like Fat Albert and Weird Harold. Roy Silver was working on a movie deal with Warners, and Cosby formed a new record label, Tetragrammaton. (Silver was delighted to get away with that name, "the unspoken name of God—look it up!") Most of the deals were happening—although one, a proposed Fat Albert hamburger chain, never got off the back burner.

Tetragrammaton was a strange label that included in its list Deep Purple and Tom Smothers' friend comic Murray Roman, and distributed the John Lennon–Yoko Ono album (with the nude cover photo) *Two Virgins* (which Bill was not thrilled with). Cosby's entry was a two-record set designed to show his "Vegas" style monologues. Instead of childhood riffs, it was an easygoing eighty minutes of Cos doing his laid-back audience-participation bits, joking about sports and gambling. He satirized gamblers who called out, "Oh God, help me" at the dice table ("Look, God has better things to do!") and shared gambling frustrations:

"I know one time I was down to my last two hundred dollars. I mean, not to my *name,* but I lost all I could sign for. And I said, 'I'm gonna win something. It can't get worse. . . .' Well, never tempt 'worse.' I went over to the roulette wheel and got two hundred dollars' worth of quarter chips. Covered the table. I mean, covered the table, red and black even up. I'm going to win something before I go to sleep. And the guy spun the ball and it fell on the floor."

He couldn't resist a little racial quip. Talking about poker chips, he said, "When we divvy up the chips, there's a way we're gonna do it: Whatever color the person, that's the color chips he's gonna get. No fair paintin' yourself."

When Cos began work on his first TV special, the network executives had a little racial quip of their own. "We don't know about this," they said. "We've got problems." Cosby was astonished. The network wanted to tuck the special out of the way, at ten P.M. Cosby wanted it on early so the kids could watch. The network stalled on a date: then the one they chose was too late to qualify for Emmy nomination that year.

Cosby remembers what one exec told him: "One of them said, 'Don't forget, Bill, you're a problem. No matter how popular you are, no matter how many kids love you, you're a problem. All black men are.' "

Years before, Cos would have pretty much let things cool out. But in these times, when his name gave him some independent clout, when people were slowly beginning to exchange the term "Negro" for "Afro-American" or "black," Cosby went to the press with some of his complaints.

In an interview with *The New York Times,* he said, "The most difficult thing is for people to accept the American Negro as a full, total human being, without him being something different."

He confronted the female reporter: "You married? Okay, then. Say I work with your husband and one day he says to me, 'Hey, man, will you go pick up my wife for me? I got something to do.' So I pick you up, and I have to put a sign on the car saying 'This woman is not my girl friend. She is married to somebody else who is also white.' "

He talked about the double standard. People were bothering him about whether he was going to have blacks and whites on his special, and it didn't matter if he said "all blacks" or "all whites" or "checkerboard." Somebody was bound to find a reason to get mad at him.

He was growing restless. "When you belong to a minority group . . . you have to walk so that you don't upset the people who are in a position to give you the next step so you can eventually walk by yourself."

For the TV special, Cosby returned to Philadelphia. The idea was to shoot some background for his street-football monologue and use actual Philly locales.

Nothing much had changed. The brick walls of the tenements were scrawled up with graffiti, trashed up with chalk marks. Cos stood out on the sidewalk in front of the buildings, smoking his cigar, watching.

There was a strange contrast on the street this day. The shabby walk-ups were all around, but in the center of the street were thousands of dollars' worth of electrical equipment, cameras, and sound recorders. And while the people gathering to watch from the sidelines were dressed poorly, the guys operating the equipment were wearing T-shirts made for the occasion, the words "The Bill Cosby Special" emblazoned across the back.

Surging forward were little kids, getting autographs from a man who was once one of them, who talked like one of them, and who was, deep inside, still one of them.

Cosby wanted some of the kids to get together and play some street football, like he remembered. But the kids who played with Cos when he was a kid didn't do it in front of TV cameras and people holding microphones and wielding lights.

The day wore on. The crew got the footage they needed. The restless crowd got a chance to praise their favorite son and envy him. Cos made a splash in the old neighborhood, and it shimmered with glory, even while a complex whirlpool of emotion stirred underneath.

Response to the special was mixed. Cosby had done the unheard of: a special without guest stars. At a time when comics hardly had any respect at all, Cos had dared to do virtually an hour of stand-up. "Mr. Cosby is very funny when he is acting out his childhood games," *The New York Times* said, "but next time the producers should remember that there are very few performers who can carry an entire show by themselves."

Over at the *Daily News,* Kay Gardella praised Cosby: "His delivery and recollections had the same universal appeal that all our great humorists manage to impart when they dip into their treasured memories of the past and its hardships, with understanding instead of resentment and anger."

Cosby, still "the experiment" in the TV world after all those triumphs, experimented with radio. Coca-Cola sponsored his five-minute daily show that gave a shot of comedy to Top 40 radio stations. Cos would appear as himself, or as characters like Brown Hornet and Captain Oh Wow, and impart unusual bits of wisdom, like "A ship without a sail has an engine in it somewhere" and "Hitch your wagon to a star and pay for it by the month."

As fast as Cosby was putting together new deals, others were unraveling. He was beginning to have conflicts with his high-pressure partners at Campbell/Silver/Cosby, and was worried about all the corporate risks. He was meeting some critical hatchets with his singing and his new comedy albums. And he was still smarting from the unexpected battles involved with putting out his comedy special.

As another hot summer threatened, with racial discontent stirring more violently than ever, Cosby journeyed to Harlem's Apollo Theater for the first time. He told the crowd, "In show business, you can be rich today and back in the projects tomorrow."

But most of the evening, which some saw as a test of how strong Cosby was without white middle-class support, turned out to be high hilarity and pure good times. Not only did the audience cheer and applaud him, even the stagehands got a special kick out of meeting their man, Alexander Scott, superspy. Bill heard two of them talking when he walked in.

"That's the cat," one whispered.

"What's he going to do?"

"I don't know, maybe shoot some cats!"

At a concert in Kansas just a few weeks later, on April 4, 1968, Cosby received the news that the Reverend Martin Luther King, Jr., had been shot.

It was hell night all over the country, a night of fear, anger, tension, and grief. Some places were burning, and some places were ready to explode. Some people were burning inside, a raging fire of pain or a flickering candle of sorrow.

Cosby's own feeling of depression began to envelop him. He'd done his first show, not yet knowing more than the sketchy rumors. Now, facing the late show, he had heard the worst. King was dead.

He remembered what had happened when President Kennedy was assassinated, the unrelieved sense of loss and hopelessness, the bitterness and the tears. Death was on everyone's lips and there was no escape. The networks shut off all regular programming and staged a twenty-four-hour wake.

Maybe some people needed escape, Cosby thought. Maybe they needed laughter, and needed it bad. It could be a healing thing. Or it could almost be sacrilege.

Bill sat in the dressing room, weary from phone conversations with a tearful Harry Belafonte, confused and depressed, as tense as all of America, wondering what would happen next.

The crowds were filing in. Time for the show. Cosby got the word: five minutes to curtain. At last he left the dressing room and made the walk toward the backstage area. He could hear the buzz out front. Then he came out onstage and the spotlights hit him.

He began to do the show, shutting off the tragedy, rambling about the crowd, and gambling, and Kansas and stuff. It wasn't working; he couldn't concentrate. He couldn't stand there in front of that small group of people when so many millions were getting the news and the news was coming fast and furious over the radio.

Cosby faltered. He'd gone as far as he could in forty minutes, and stopped. He told his fans that he couldn't continue.

The audience was stunned.

Slowly, they began to applaud. The applause reached a crescendo, swelling louder, until it seemed they couldn't applaud enough. The audience stood as one, standing and applauding.

And they let Cos go, audience and performer sharing a moment of understanding and pain, and wondering what the rest of the nation would do with their own sense of loss.

Back in the dressing room, the calls were coming in. He was going to meet with Belafonte in Memphis. A call came from Robert Culp. The two of them were going to go down together, and be part of the Memphis march.

After Memphis, Cosby went to Atlanta for the funeral. Famous faces were there, but changed somehow by the moment—no longer looking like stars, just worn-out people. Along with Cosby, there were Stevie Wonder, Robert Kennedy, Ossie Davis, and Ruby Dee. There were Dizzy Gillespie and Lena Horne, and all the people who had worked with Dr. King, marched with King, and were now marching for what was left of the dream.

Bill took it all in, the long ceremony marked with ripples of anger in the heartache, fury in the frustration. He stayed until the speeches began. When the politicians started to voice their profound sense of shock, and their heartfelt sympathies, he quietly slipped away.

Some time later, Cosby received a letter from Robert Kennedy about the King assassination. He had it framed and hung on his office wall, near the framed copy of the Emancipation Proclamation and a sculpture of Dr. King.

In June, Cosby appeared in an episode of the seven-part CBS series *Of Black America.* In a fourth-grade classroom at the Old Tarrytown Road School in New York, Cosby and the teacher, Mrs. Lovely Billups, talked with the kids about black history.

"When I was growing up, we didn't get information about anybody but the usual people," Cosby recalled later. "Of course we learned how the Ku Klux Klan rode in and separated families. We lived in a ghetto, what must have been Philadelphia's first housing project—ninety-nine and nine-tenths percent black. I don't know whether any white person can imagine how that feels."

Cosby hoped to tell people more about black history and black leaders, and to "erase the stereotypes about what the black man is." And he remembered his vow to return to school, and to find ways of teaching the children.

"I think there's a lot to be said for fighting at the blackboard, with a piece of chalk as a weapon."

Chapter
10

For his first solo TV series, NBC wanted Cosby to be a comical detective, but he wanted to play a schoolteacher.

"OK," they said, "how about playing a schoolteacher who moonlights at night as a detective?"

"How about I just play a schoolteacher?" Cos said.

NBC gave in. After all, Cosby had another option—he could continue his studies and *become* a schoolteacher, just as he was saying he would do someday. They still wondered what kind of wild, zany sitcom plots his show would have.

His answer: none. No inane characters, no farce, and no booming laugh track. "The character I play will do certain things that will provoke anger," he told writer Kay Gardella. He will be "a human being: He makes mistakes, gets into trouble, and reflects quite frequently on the human condition. . . . What I'm really doing is a study of human behavior. My actions will be deplorable sometimes, but by being that way I'm saying to an audience, 'Are you really that pure?' My character will do all those things a person does when eyes aren't on him. He'll put his feet up on the desk, jump on the trampoline with his shoes on, and frequently act out of selfish motives."

One of the writers on the series was Ed Weinberger, who had been at Central High in Philly at the same time as Cosby. Preparing for the show, he noted, "People identify with Bill's humor because it's an honest admission of his vulnerability. He is happy to be vulnerable. It's a confession of his humanity."

With the premiere show scheduled for September of 1969, Cosby finished up some of his other projects, like a TV special called "As I See

It," in which ten children got a chance to make their own eight-milli-
meter movies and show them, with Cos as host.

Executive producer for the *NBC Children's Theatre* project, George
Heinemann, couldn't say enough about working with Cosby. "Boy, he's
very much Mr. Casual. The kids love him, and obviously he loves the
kids." Working with Cosby was child's play: "He invites us up to his
house, and we sit around about three and one-half hours, have something to eat, chat about the good old days—his in Philly—and he listens
to suggestions about how we think the show ought to go." And off it
went.

Cosby had pretty much the same approach to his appearances on *The
Tonight Show.* He'd become a popular guest host starting back in January 1965. At that time, the *New York Herald Tribune* wrote, "Johnny
Carson had best look to his squat-and-chat laurels," because Cosby's
show, with Art Carney and Jason Robards, Jr., aboard, "was one of the
better late shows in many a moon."

Cos no longer did set routines, preferring relaxed ad-libs. He says the
change happened in the midst of a preplanned bit: "The audience
started laughing at something . . . and I didn't know what was funny
or why they were laughing, so I just started talking about something.
And it turned out to be very, very funny . . . ever since then I've just
been walking out and talking," mixing spontaneous observation with
occasional lines from his nightclub act.

Things looked cool and calm when Cosby began guest-host duties
one week in March 1968. Monday and Tuesday nights' shows went fine.
Then on Wednesday night, March 19, Cos rambled through his monologue, including a few lines about visiting a Catholic church for the first
time. His wife was Catholic, of course, and helped him understand the
different rituals. But he couldn't quite figure out the wafers, those "individual pizzas."

Meanwhile, at the NBC switchboard, they couldn't understand why
the room had gotten about one hundred watts brighter. The board was
lit up with an overflow of four hundred calls.

For the first time, Cosby found himself swept up into coast-to-coast
controversy on a matter of taste. With those two words, "individual
pizzas," the gentle, modern Mark Twain was branded as the worst kind
of villain. How could the man prey on a defenseless minority group!

Eleanor Roberts, a columnist for the *Boston Herald Traveler,* was one
of the many writers who felt that Cos had "done serious damage to his
image. I don't buy this nonsense of *The Tonight Show* reaching a more

liberal and sophisticated audience. That excuse is not open sesame to mock any religious faith." Pointing out that NBC had bleeped out a pair of curses (a hell and a damn, or perhaps it was two damns), Roberts charged "they took infinite care to delete two swear words . . . but they gave the green light to a blasphemy that won't soon be forgotten."

Papers all over the country picked up on the anti-Catholic attack from Bill Cosby. It was a sober, self-controlled young man who faced the cameras the following night and said, "I want to apologize for those offended by the routine. . . ."

Standing on the chalk mark and watching his step, he chose his words carefully. "I was merely giving an outsider's viewpoint toward religion in humorous terms," he said. "But I guess you can't do that on TV."

Ironically, when Bill's second annual comedy special ran barely two weeks later, it included a bit of biblical humor (his famous Noah routine, this time acted out with Cos in costume, complete with white beard) and a reference to his and Fat Albert's visit to church: "The coolest part was putting Scotch tape backwards on the fingernails and waiting for the collection plate to come around."

As with his first special, Cosby had no guest stars, carrying the entire show virtually alone. He did introduce someone sitting out in the audience—his mom. She called up to him, "Are you saving your money?"

The special received positive reviews, and Cosby was encouraged, hoping that fans of his simple, human style of comedy would respond to his new, low-key TV series.

The first episode of the show was a slice-of-life study of Cos as Chet (only his mother called him Chester) Kincaid, enjoying his day off from teaching phys. ed. About the most exciting thing that happened was that a pair of cops pulled him over while he was jogging, thinking he might be a neighborhood prowler.

Variety was not pleased with the mild show, to put it mildly. With most premieres coming out running, "Cosby came out jogging. His preem episode was frail and contrived . . . short on humor and even shorter on story, and it was pointless besides. Presumably the intention is to key the scripts to the kind of fanciful anecdote that is the main stuff of Cosby's stand-up routines. The danger in that . . . is (1) that Cosby's tales may be better heard than seen and (2) that five minutes' worth of airy material may not stretch to a half hour."

It looked like Cosby's show was a prime candidate for quick cancellation. It just wasn't frantic, as most sitcoms of the era were.

At least nobody seemed to be bringing up the racial issue. Cos had jumped that hurdle with *I Spy,* and the year before it had been Diahann Carroll's turn. As the first black to star in a sitcom, she took the same flack Cosby had for being an "unrealistic" role model, a cute, middle-class black who dared to act equal to and just like whites.

Diahann's show, *Julia,* even included lines that naïvely suggested that some of the racial conflicts were over—or at least that the sight of a black face was no cause for alarm, as it had been when *I Spy* first came on the scene. In the opening episode, when Julia applies for a job, she tells the gruff-looking employer (Lloyd Nolan), "I'm colored. I'm a Negro." He hires her as a nurse anyway, answering, "Have you always been a Negro, or are you just trying to be fashionable?"

Julia was still on the air when Cosby's show turned up. Cosby could breathe a little easy. Maybe critics could attack him for being cute and mild, but now at least the question was about the comedy and not "the Problem." He had risen above it, with dignity, just as he'd planned.

Then a huge article by Faith Berry appeared in *The New York Times.* Bill Cosby was a cop-out, a disappointment to the black community. The *Times* criticized him for being "easy-going, likable, and at times too farcical to be true; he's everybody's friend, usually all the time."

Berry wanted to know why Cosby's show didn't contain the racial strife of *To Sir with Love* or *Blackboard Jungle.* She was furious that the situation comedy had not covered "Afro-American history, community control of schools, teacher strikes, the black family, the black neighborhood, the busing of school children . . . soul culture."

How dare Bill Cosby show a middle-class black? And how about the family of Chet Kincaid? Why was it that Chet's brother works driving a garbage truck but "we've certainly seen nothing about the plight of any black garbage worker on this show." Grudgingly, Berry allowed that the show was saying "blacks are human," but surely Cosby could do more than that.

It also seemed to gall *The New York Times* that this mild-mannered sitcom, which didn't seem to have *any* chance at all opposite *The Ed Sullivan Show* and *The F.B.I.,* was currently number one among the season's new shows. "It will probably remain a popular show, since many white viewers will continue to watch it because they find it refreshing. Blacks will do likewise, still hoping to identify with it."

In Hollywood, Cos quietly continued his work on the show. He kept the anger inside. "I help black people in my own way," he said. "It's just that I don't talk about it." He was tired of defending his philosophy to foolish white reporters and ax-grinding black ones. He didn't call attention to the fact that half the crew on *The Bill Cosby Show* was black, or that large numbers of blacks were getting their big acting breaks on the show, or that many episodes had all-black casts. This was *years* before the premieres of *Sanford and Son* and *The Jeffersons*.

The Bill Cosby Show ended up number eleven for the season, just behind such superstars of American comedy as Red Skelton and Lucille Ball, and ahead of powerhouse programs hosted by Carol Burnett and Dean Martin. Not bad for a quiet, human little show about a person Faith Berry considered "a kind of half-man who, had he lived in the days of Nat Turner, might have sold Turner down the river."

Once again, Cosby's humor turned people around, and his own personal philosophy in comedy was vindicated. *The New York Times* was then quick to run an article the exact opposite of the first. Another black writer, A. S. Doc Young, came to bury Berry, not to praise her:

"Bill Cosby, through sheer force of personality and great talent, has created a hit show, perhaps an improbable hit show. . . . Cosby looms tall among hero figures for black kids who need hero figures in the worst way. . . . Meanwhile, he relates in a constructive way to millions of adult viewers of all races. . . . Cosby would not be at his best as a professional civil rights leader, a Black Panther, or the head of a poverty program. But as Bill Cosby—comic, wit, humorist, and storyteller—he is making an important contribution to Afro-Americans, to Americans as a whole. His contribution is not to be taken lightly."

While he continued to overcome prejudice by simply proving his race-neutral equality, Cosby used a light touch on his show, one of the hardest things to pull off in comedy. When asked what was the most difficult style of comedy to write, veteran comedy writer Hal Kanter answered, "Subtlety. Innuendo." He said it was far easier to write zany humor or insult humor à la Redd Foxx, where you say "the most common, childish, aggressive statements and the audiences scream at them."

Instead, Cosby's writers aimed for realism and for character comedy. One show was simply a study of Chet's reactions to a neighbor's barking dog, who is keeping him awake nights. The neighbor is a comely young black girl—so Chet tries to be pleasant and friendly, even to the dog. But when he sees the panting animal, its tongue flapping in and out of its mouth, he grumbles, "You're making me tired, the way you breathe, you know that, don't ya?" As usual, any Cosby hostility translates into comic observation.

Chet tries everything to get to sleep, including wearing headphones and "sleep socks," but the yapping dog never stops. With a numb smile on his face, his eyes glassy, Chet eventually falls asleep with his eyes open during an important conference, snoring lightly.

A Dick Van Dyke would've done a rubber-band dance of exhaustion. Lucille Ball might've swooned into a dead sleep on top of everybody. Redd Foxx would've gone after the barking dog with a shotgun. But here, subtly and realistically, Chet just nods out, producing memorable chuckles. In fact, realism was so important to the show that even physical details were authentic: Perhaps for the first time on TV, a sitcom character went to bed not in neat, starched pajamas buttoned up to the neck, but in a pair of undershorts.

Also, unlike most sitcoms, some episodes presented the star in an unflattering light.

When a halfback on the football team is so hyped on winning that he gets into fights when he loses, Chet lectures him: "The important thing is not winning. It's knowing what to do when you lose. Humility in victory; pride in defeat."

It's a nice speech, but Chet doesn't practice what he preaches. Competing in a handball tournament, he tries all kinds of sneaky tricks to win: cheap distractions ("Your sneakers don't look like they fit you"); pleas for sympathy ("My back's sore today"); and irritating ploys, like asking "Are you ready?" before every serve. And when he ultimately loses the tourney to a player who uses the same unsavory tactics, Chet becomes angry and sullen, argues with the referee, and storms off the court.

The student is shocked. "Mr. Kincaid acts just the way I do when I lose. It's kind of silly, isn't it? Now I see how I look and, believe me, I'm gonna change."

The student changes, but Chet remains the same! After forcing himself to finally congratulate the new champ, Chet slinks away insulting him behind his back.

Cosby told his writers: "There are times when Chet will miss the point. He may be looking for something and it may be right in front of his nose. I do this deliberately, figuring that people will identify with Chet and become better teachers, better mothers, better fathers."

Chet wasn't always infallible with kids, either. In one episode (which featured an early TV appearance by Lou Gossett, Jr.), he tries to persuade some neighborhood kids to play basketball instead of hanging out on the sidewalk. When one kid tells Chet to get lost, he says, "Whatsa matter, nobody ever been nice to ya?"

The kid's heart is not warmed. "Here," the little boy says, walking away with his friends, "I'll leave the whole sidewalk to you in my will."

Of course, episodes showing the warmth of human nature and recognizable character comedy were more typical. Chet takes over his nephew's paper route, grandly proclaiming, "There's no labor a man can do that's undignified—if he does it right." He arrives at the newspaper truck at five A.M. only to be eyed suspiciously by the other paperboys and by the man handing out the papers.

"How do I *know* you're taking your nephew's place?" the man asks solemnly. "You got some identification?"

"Why," Chet pleads, "would I be here at six in the morning? What am I gonna do with forty newspapers?"

"Maybe," the man answers slowly, "you like to read."

At last Chet convinces the man, who says a line that kids have been hearing ever since parents and teachers were invented: "Tell ya what I'm gonna do. I'm gonna take a chance on ya. Don't let me down."

The rest of the episode involves Chet's misadventures delivering papers—to all the wrong houses—and trying to get them back again from crabby neighbors and vicious dogs.

Cosby's show was a great place for black technicians and crewmen, as well as many black actors and actresses, to find employment. Cosby's brother Russell was even around, studying to become a cameraman. But the show also offered young kids a chance to break into show business. The corridors of Richard Allen Holmes High (a reference, of course, to Cosby's home at the Richard Allen projects of Philadelphia) were filled with students—like Ed Begley, Jr., and a young Mark Hamill, who got to deliver the immortal line, "All right, you goons, you've had your fun. Cool it!"

Some episodes of the show were, as some critics claimed, a little preachy or slow-moving. One was nothing more than a history lesson (Chet teaching an Hispanic carpenter enough to become a citizen), coupled with a civics lesson (the carpenter stands up at the show's end to recite his version of the Bill of Rights—"People are people . . . they should be free and happy").

But more often the care and effort that went into these seemingly slim plots paid off. For example, one episode had Elsa Lanchester as an eccentric lady bent on preserving trees. "Save one tree and you will breathe easier," Chet says, giving her a slogan. But despite all their efforts, the duo can't save one little tree that stands in the way of construction at a building site.

Most of the episode had been involved with all the ways to try and save the tree, from protests to newspaper publicity, and possible transplantation. But when it's destroyed, the episode poignantly stands still for a moment. Then Chet and the lady are seen out on the highway, planting new trees. Chet tells a skeptical kid that, aside from shade and oxygen, it's important to have trees "as home base in hide-and-seek."

Buoyed by the ratings, Bill and the writers tried to experiment with new techniques in putting together a sitcom in keeping with his strong intent on educating, with valuable lessons that kids could put into practice themselves. Cosby, as Chet Kincaid, handled diverse problems: peer pressure from a baseball team when their star player, an Orthodox Jew, refuses to play on Saturday; teaching a girl how to drive a car without fear by using a lot of reverse psychology.

Typical Cosby comic dialogue turned up in an episode about the cafeteria's poor menu. He tells the pretty black manager, "We all have to give up a little authority in the face of liberty. They want an end to the liver chow mein . . . and they want the tomato surprise not to be such a big surprise. They want an end to chipped beef on toast with creamed gravy and raisins."

"I think raisins help," she says.

"Dear, nothing helps chipped beef on toast."

There was room to experiment with all types of comedy, even the kind of funky black humor that would be the keystone of *Sanford and Son* a few years later. In one episode, Cosby used two of the greatest comedians of black vaudeville, Mantan Moreland and Moms Mabley. Cast as Uncle Dewey and Aunt Edna, they played a raucous, fighting couple.

"When a man starts to get old," Moms rasps, "get rid of him! He can't do nothin', won't do nothin', and don't want *you* to do nothin'!" Pointing at Mantan, she thunders, "There's a man that gets out of breath puttin' his pajamas on at night! That's a man who has to take naps so he can be rested when he goes to sleep!"

Moreland's gravelly comeback: "I wouldn't keep my eyes closed so much if my eyes had something to look at. I used to stay home from work just to avoid kissin' you good-bye."

Moms shouts, "He snores so loud it rattles my teeth!"

Mantan yells, "Then you should keep 'em in a glass farther from the bed!"

The episode showed that Cosby had respect for the old-time comedians and their ethnic character comedy, even if he wasn't willing or able to perform it himself. But through the coming decade, he not only would have to find ways of keeping his own style of comedy current and fresh, he would have to weather an upheaval in the humor of black comedians.

Into the turbulent late sixties and early seventies, there would be the change from *Negro* to *Afro-American* to *black*. Along the way, the black community had convulsions over what was funny and why. Redd Foxx and Sherman Hemsley would veer toward reverse racism, becoming black Archie Bunkers. Flip Wilson would do overtly ethnic characters like Geraldine, and Jimmie Walker would become the dummy funster of *Good Times.* All would be accused, by various black factions, of damaging black pride, of not being black enough, of not being funny, or even of being too funny. And at the center of attention would be still another black comic, Richard Pryor, the "crazy nigger" whose stinging barbs would alarm some blacks and whites, and titillate others.

Would Bill Cosby try to navigate, as he had in the sixties, the bewildering, swirling waters of social change just to get a few laughs?

Cosby had some other plans. He had a home in Amherst, Massachusetts, and he was taking courses. There was the lure of retirement to the good life, of becoming a teacher, and of dumping all the controversy of his career. Voted Man of the Year in 1969 by the Harvard University Hasty Pudding Club (Paul Newman won in 1968, and Robert Redford would win in 1970), Cos could end his career on a high note.

And what about his kids? Ennis William arrived April 15, 1969, and there was a great temptation to stay home and watch him and the others grow. Even though he'd spent most of his past two years in California, Camille told him once, "You only see them six or seven months out of the year, and yet you know their personalities so well." But how much better could he know them if he was home more often? The children, Cosby said, "accept that they have a father who must travel for his work, but who comes home. That's the important thing. They know it's a job and I'll be back." Maybe it was time to come back for good.

Chapter

11

Cosby's dream home was a farm outside Amherst where he could raise his family and also work on his studies at the University of Massachusetts. More and more, he was drawn to the country life, and as his TV series faded, he told more and more people that his goal was to become a real teacher.

The 135-year-old clapboard farmhouse had cost $64,000 initially, but renovations siphoned off an additional $325,000 from the Cosby bank account. The sixteen-room house had five working stone fireplaces, making it especially cozy on those snowy New England nights—Cos had missed the snow during all those years living in the thirty-one-room California mansion he'd dubbed the "Cosby Hilton."

There weren't as many guests coming by as in the old days, but there was always room for old California friends like Clarence Williams III, or new ones, like pianist-composer Eubie Blake.

The country life, in both summer and winter, appealed to Bill. Fantasists might even say that it recalled the stories of Huckleberry Finn and Tom Sawyer that his mother read him as a boy, only instead of the Mississippi River, there was the nearby Connecticut River. In the summer, he could use the tennis court or commune with nature, go for walks on the 286-acre grounds with specially planted flower beds and fruit trees. In the winter, great fun could be had with old-fashioned sleigh rides, playing with the kids, or simply enjoying the serenity of a landscape gracefully covered in snow.

A quiet place, Cosby's estate was sufficiently off the beaten track to discourage tourists and fans. And it was far enough away from the local public schools—twenty-two miles—that Camille had to get up at six in the morning to drive the kids in each day.

Of the two small barns on the property, one was converted into an office for Cosby, and the other became a home for Cosby's mom. The place became more and more of a seductive, permanent home with each improvement and with the further acquisition of expensive period antiques.

The kids went to school, and so did Cos, in his own way. It was informal at first. The University of Massachusetts had a flexible program for their master's student. First of all, they admitted him even though he hadn't finished his four years at Temple, feeling he'd qualified on the basis of "life experience." (Temple would later gather up Cosby's massive volume of work and translate it into a bachelor of arts degree.) Second, because he was studying the link between television and education, he had to be free to work on projects in New York and Hollywood, like his *Fat Albert* cartoon specials, documentaries, and *The Electric Company.*

The Electric Company, aimed at bettering the reading skills of seven-to-ten-year-olds, was the perfect vehicle for Cosby's whimsical instructional talents. He could help teach kids how *d* could turn *be* into *bed* and, in song, demonstrate the value of the "Double E":

"Oh, you can flee to Tennessee for a three-day spree! Have yourself a time at a jamboree! Anywhere you go you find you can't get free from Double E!"

The Electric Company seems taken for granted now, along with *Sesame Street,* but back in the early seventies it was an exciting breakthrough, something Bill was keen to become involved with even though he was sacrificing a lot of time and a lot of money. Skip Hinnant, one of the regulars on the show, recalls, "None of us were getting rich on the show and I know Cosby wasn't getting anything like his normal salary. He was intensely interested in the show as a new idea in reading. We had a research team working on the techniques for teaching, and for every dollar we spent in production they spent five in research, finding out what worked and what didn't."

Cos was magic on the set. Everyone called him either Cos or Bill, and right from the start, Skip recalls, "Bill was very open, very unpretentious. And he had the biggest collection of sneakers in the world! This was before running shoes became a fad. He'd come in with some leather sneaks or new tennis shoes and say, 'Look at these, Skip, look at these!' And I'd want to go out and buy a pair, or he'd bring me a pair. That's all he ever wore, jeans and sneakers.

"During the first year we didn't know what would work and what wouldn't, but he was laid-back and even-tempered even in the toughest times. It was eighteen-hour days, getting out of the studio at nine or ten at night.

"He was very cool about all that. I could imagine other stars saying, 'The hell with this, I'm goin' home, not for this kind of money am I gonna stay here till ten after coming in at seven in the morning.' But if he felt it had to be done, he worked as hard as the next."

Of course, Cos was not about to play "nice guy" *all* the time. He stood up for himself. "If he felt a sketch wasn't up to his standards, he'd say, 'I'm not going to spend a lot of time on this, just so you know up front. Let's get it done quick.' Or he'd say, 'This thing sucks, why don't we punch it up? Let's improvise.' " And Cos and the crew would cut loose and have some fun ad-libbing new lines. Though it was a monitored and carefully devised experiment, *The Electric Company* did provide ample opportunity for improvisation, and some of the best sketches were total ad-libs.

"He was a lot of fun on the set," Skip says. "He can be very casual and funny, but he has great dignity, too. You know you don't screw around with him, but at the same time you know you can."

To this day Bill enjoys the reputation of someone who loves to giggle, laugh, keep things loose—but keep enough respect and seriousness that when it's time to work, the fooling around ends.

There was plenty of Billfoolery on the *Electric Company* set. When Camille would come in for a visit, Bill loved to tease her in front of cast and crew. "He'd try to embarrass her to death," Skip Hinnant chuckles, "but Camille was cool. He'd flirt with somebody, and clown around, but Camille was still cool. A very, very even-tempered lady." Bill was literally a circus ringleader for silliness. Once when the entire cast was dressed up in clown makeup and costumes, Bill said, "Okay, everybody! Let's go out for dinner!" And suddenly a fancy nearby restaurant, Oscar's Salt of the Sea, was besieged by a bunch of crazy clowns, startling guests just by standing around with their happiest smiles on and their gaudiest, brightest outfits.

Harmless shocks for adults were only a part of Bill's impishness. One day some kids recognized him as he was leaving the studio. He smiled at them, began to jog, and then broke into a frantic dead run. The kids shrieked and raced after him, and for two blocks he led a ragtag, ever-growing group of giggling, laughing children on a merry chase. Finally Bill crashed into a trash can and went rolling over and over. The kids pounced on him, and there was a good-natured roughhouse right there on the street.

"He loves that kind of thing," Skip recalls with a smile. "It's real-life humor. It's funny and alive, and that's why I think everything he does works so well."

Cos kept up with the show for two full seasons, at the same time maintaining his own adult education studies. His new-found interest in education did clash with his old, long-standing frustration with school-work. Describing his studies at the University of Massachusetts, he said, "You look at things, and you say, 'Gee whiz, this is interesting, all these things. . . .' Then you find out, 'Gee whiz, this is going to take me eight hundred years before I'm finished with this!' "

The more involved Cos became in the academic community, the more inactive he was in mainstream entertainment projects. But as 1971 was drawing to a close, so was some of the comedian's enthusiasm for the sequestered life of academia. "I was starting to feel like I was ac-complishing nothing. Nobody was pushing me. It's just that I seemed to lack something."

Cos went out on more club dates. He shared his traditional stories of childhood, but also included new material that seemed to reflect Chet Kincaid (a routine about playing handball and getting wiped out by a cool old man who just walked to the right spot, hit the ball the right way, and drove him nuts). He also did a bit about one of his most embarrassing moments, a visit with Ray Charles.

"Some people have their thoughts about what stars are like—like they never make a mistake. But have you ever been in a position where you were saying something and you *knew* that it was dumb? Totally without question just dumb? And as you got halfway through it your brain said *dumb, dumb, dumb* . . . but your mouth kept rattling it off?" Bill came up to Ray's suite. "I go up, and I walk in. Now, the lights are *out.* It's pitch black in this apartment. And I said, 'Ray, where are you?' He said, 'I'm in the bathroom, shaving.' So I said, 'Well, Ray, why are you shaving in the dark'—and I tried to stop it right there, but the rest of it came—'with the lights out?' Dumb! Dumb! Brainless human being!

"Ray was very nice about it. He said, 'I've been shaving in the dark all my life.' I tried to cover, 'Aw, I was just jokin', Ray . . . bet ya have a low electric bill, doncha . . . ?' "

As Cos made the rounds of the nightclubs, and as *I Spy* and *The Bill*

Cosby Show turned up in reruns, Cosby still wanted to do something more, something different. Something he hadn't tried before.

How about movies? How about Bill Cosby becoming the next Warren Beatty?

Bill's film career *could* have started that way. Back in 1969, Cosby was scheduled to star in his first movie—*Heaven Can Wait.*

Bill's manager, Roy Silver, was crazy about the movie, which was originally made in 1941 as *Here Comes Mr. Jordan.* He even owned a sixteen-millimeter print of it. When the money started coming in, Roy bought the film rights with his own money—$250,000. He thought it would be great for Cosby. He'd play a black man who dies and comes back to earth in a rich white man's body. The viewer sees Cosby as he really is, but everybody else sees him—and treats him differently— because he appears to be an aristocrat.

Imagine *Heaven Can Wait* starring Bill Cosby—with a screenplay by Francis Ford Coppola. The script was ready, the project was paid for, but by the time Cosby was free to do the movie, he and Silver had split up. Now Cosby had to find a different film. He chose *Man and Boy.*

Cosby, presiding over Jemmin Incorporated along with Marvin Miller (who had produced Bill's TV show), found that the machinery that seemed to work pretty well for Silver/Campbell/Cosby was a bit gummy. Producer Miller told *Variety* about the problems in getting the project off the ground. "It's been intimated to me that this is not the kind of picture that people will buy today. It's a very old-fashioned picture, a family picture . . . a typical Disney-type picture, the story of a man's dignity and his love for his family."

Cosby's name, which meant three Emmy Awards and five Grammy Awards, didn't mean a thing in the land of the Oscars. Bill had no reputation in movies and was coming off only a mild success in television. His records for the Uni label were not the million-sellers the early Warners efforts were.

Miller discovered that movie executives weren't buying the concept of a black family's trials out West after the Civil War. One told him, "How can you make a film like this, when there *were* no black cowboys?" Besides, nobody in the movie was going to shed their blood or their clothes.

Cosby had determination, something the studios didn't understand. He had the courage of his convictions—something else the studios didn't understand. And he had money enough to start making the film himself. *That* the studios really didn't understand.

"Friends, with tears in their eyes, said, 'If you don't get a studio to put up the money, don't make the picture,' " Bill recalled. "There were just enough no's that I didn't like, the kind of reasons given that are why black actors don't act, black directors don't direct, and black writers don't write as far as the screen is concerned." Cosby told people he would go ahead.

His foremost supporter was Camille. She saw him brooding about the problem, spending hours on the phone, brightening with every glimmer of a promise, only to sink back when the answer was no. She told him to go ahead, even though he was risking the family's savings.

In Scottsdale, Arizona, Cosby and a forty-member crew set up shop. There was optimism, but also tension. This would be a race. They were starting a picture but weren't sure if it would ever be completed. They were racing against time, against money, hoping to find a backer before Cosby's bankroll gave out. Cos counseled his cast and crew that they were going to do the best job they could, as long as they could.

Visitors to the set couldn't believe it. Every step of the way Cosby seemed to be making success impossible. The script called for a villain, the perfect spot for a big name to help at the box office. But Cos rewrote the part for Douglas Turner Ward.

"The original script had a white guy in the role, but we changed that. Bob Culp and I have done the black-white thing in *I Spy* as well as most movies have, I think, and I've had that. This confrontation between two black men is not only a fresh approach but real and a lot more dramatic. And why not have a good black actor playing a heavy?"

There would be no splashy black-white gimmick on this picture.

Cosby and the crew kept going, full tilt, treating the project like the quality motion picture they wanted it to be. No short cuts, no cheap shots. A porno movie can be made for under $75,000, even today. A quickie horror movie could be done for under $200,000. But here was Cosby, his film already costing $350,000.

Hardly a month into the project, they'd managed to put together some first-rate scenes. Marvin Miller took every scrap of film he could get his hands on, and kept trying to make a last-minute deal.

The ready cash was running out. Was this going to be another scene out of North Philly, with Cosby and his family being threatened with eviction because they couldn't pay?

Cosby began hearing from people who would back his movie. But they were offering the con—like bringing a TV set to a poor family in the ghetto—with a contract and a lot of fine print. One was going to give him the money—in return for being named Cosby's manager. Another promised to back the movie for a 70–30 split of the profits and, in fine print, a cut of his subsequent nightclub work and album sales. They figured Cos was on a tightrope, ready to fall into their safety net, even with all those strings attached.

Cosby had learned the business; he didn't fall for the con. He worked without salary, as did Marvin Miller, and he kept putting all his energies into the project. Sequestered in his office near the Scottsdale set, he heard a knock on the door. "Hey Bill," one of his young fans called. "Come out and play!"

Cos paused, and answered, "I can't today, man. I gotta stay in and study."

While he was trying to find an answer to the financial problems, one of his co-stars, Leif Erickson, had to handle a problem of his own. Erickson had gotten word that his son had been killed in an accident.

Numbed with grief, the actor stood firm, remaining on the set to finish his part in the *Man and Boy* project. Between takes, the shattered father was weeping, but when the cameras were on him, he went through his lines without a mistake, to the awe of the entire crew.

"I can honestly say that this has been the most stimulating, the best thing I have ever been associated with," Cosby declared. "Only one-fifth of the picture has been put together and I am convinced that it is going to be a winner."

Finally somebody else was convinced. A white businessman had screened segments from *Man and Boy* and gave Marvin Miller the go-ahead. Cosby could now concentrate more on his acting than on his frenzied behind-the-scenes production work.

The basic story of *Man and Boy* chronicles the efforts of Caleb (Cosby) to set up a home for his wife (played by Clarence Williams III's real-life bride, Gloria Foster) and his son (George Spell). When the boy sneaks off to ride the family's horse, Caleb is worried. The horse is the family's life, the hardest-working and most valuable thing they have. While in the boy's care, the horse is stolen.

In the face of this cruel, discouraging blow, man and boy stay together as a unit, and begin the search for their horse, a long trek that tests their stamina, their dignity, and their love.

Caleb is forced to take menial jobs along the way, and he and his son must endure the hard work and the harsh insults of others, including a rowdy ranch hand (Yaphet Kotto), who delights in belittling the father in front of his child. Caleb must also handle the gunman who stole the horse (Douglas Turner Ward) and vigilantes who accuse him of horse theft himself.

Throughout *Man and Boy,* family life and the things that keep a family strong are underscored. The rugged problems faced by the pioneer family (including having to sleep three to a bed, and fight against those trying to take away their meager shelter) are meant to mirror problems faced by urban families. The family bonds are tested in every way possible. A test of love and devotion is shown in one sequence when Caleb meets up with a comely widow (Miriam Colon) who offers her board and bed, much to the son's confusion and disapproval. And idyllic moments come, too, with the father and son living off the land, shooting birds for food, building a fire, taking care of each other against the elements.

The end result was applauded for its honesty, and Cosby was praised for his dedication to his purpose. "The plight of the black man in the frontier West is a wonderfully provocative film theme," *The New York Times* wrote at the time. "It puts Mr. Cosby on first base in screen drama." The *San Francisco Chronicle* wrote, "Cosby's role is believable and fresh with no cardboard heroes."

For a family picture, an unpopular item when only R-rated films seemed to draw people away from their TV sets, *Man and Boy* didn't do too badly. A maverick production without a big studio push, it didn't receive the distribution it should have gotten.

Bill had no time to brood over the box-office figures for *Man and Boy.* He was seriously involved with other noncomedy projects. The previous year he had narrated a documentary, "Give Us the Children," about the problems faced by school systems in the inner cities. Now he was determined to go forward as a spokesman for a number of causes involving both children and inner-city life.

On June 18, 1971, Bill attended a dinner given to support the Congressional Black Caucus, honoring the election of such black members of Congress as Ronald Dellums, Charles Rangel, and Shirley Chisholm. Here was another side of Bill Cosby, one seldom seen by the public.

"Good evening," Cos opened. "I think all you niggers . . ."

The audience erupted into gales of surprised laughter. "I say good evening, niggers, because that's what a lot of you are gonna be when you leave this room. And I mean the white people sittin' there too. Niggers come in all colors."

When the applause died down, he continued, "I'm going to support the caucus as long as I live. I'll support 'em because the black establishment for too long has been the entertainers. The black entertainers very seldom get to enjoy what white entertainers have . . . that is, to be able to go out on the Riviera with sunglasses and float around on a raft. . . . No, 'cause if you saw a picture of me on a raft with sunglasses on you'd say, 'Look at that nigger and we up here strugglin'!' You wouldn't even give me a chance to tell you I was floatin' on that raft for y'all!"

Cosby spoke about the need for black solidarity. Referring to the impassioned speech of the previous speaker, he said, "Ossie Davis just left here, poured his heart and soul into a beautiful speech so you could make the sign, give a half-hour handshake to each other and walk out and still be a nigger. . . . You don't need speakers to tell you every day who you are and where you have to go and who's cheating you. And you have to stop blaming people. Can't blame the Jew who owns the store—'We oughta go over there and take his store'—'cause there ain't but seven of you in this place can run a store!"

Over the laughter, Cosby told the audience to support black politicians and performers: "Ray Charles can't make the money he used to make 'cause Joe Cocker's doin' it. You can't blame white people. Who are *you* paying your money to support and see? When you leave here, it depends on just how long it takes you before you go back to being a nigger."

And finally, he told the audience to educate their kids. "It's got to start with the young." He talked about the drug problem. "Kids taking dope today. They were taking it yesterday. Only reason why anybody knows about it now is that white kids are involved in it heavily."

Cosby's involvement in the anti drug movement included a TV special on March 27, 1971, called "Bill Cosby Talks with Children about Drugs," which was aimed at kids thinking about using drugs. "The time spent acquiring a drug habit and kicking it is time you could have used to educate yourself," he said. "Every person I have ever known who developed a bad habit spent most of the rest of his life trying to kick it, staying with it, or never using it forever." On his *Bill Cosby Talks to Kids about Drugs* album, he sang songs about the effect of speed and downers, and underscored the theme, "Dope is for the dopies." At a time when there was virtually nothing out there, Cosby was ahead of his time in calling attention to the problem.

Kids listened because Cosby listened to them. "I listen," he said, "and I answer them just as seriously as possible. And if I don't know the answer, I'll tell them I don't know."

Aside from his antidrug work, Cos was chairman of the National

Hemophilia Foundation, raised money for the American Cancer Society, VISTA, the American Heart Association, and others. The money he made from doing a toothpaste commercial went to the American Fund for Dental Education, an organization designed to help black students pursue careers in dentistry.

In the midst of all this, Cos was working on TV specials, even one in which he played Aesop and told animated fables to a pair of children. He was also out on the road, doing stand-up gigs around the country. But something was wrong. Cosby seemed to sense it. Stand-up comedy was the cornerstone of his career, the very foundation. But it was cracking in two.

Chapter

12

There were two Bill Cosbys in stand-up. There was the childlike comic that kids loved, who talked about how horrible parents were. But now there was the Vegas comic, Cosby the parent, the adult talking about how horrible kids were.

A schizophrenic rip produced two very different Bill Cosbys, and the difference was magnified with the release of two albums, *When I Was a Kid* and *For Adults Only*. And the question was whether anybody was even going to listen.

The first, *When I Was a Kid,* sees Cos in his all-too-familiar role of storytelling nostalgist. Cosby always resented being labeled a "nostalgia" act: "It's larger than nostalgia. A lot of drama is going on up there. This is storytelling, one of the great lost arts of our time. It's not all, 'Oh yeah, I remember that.' Man, nobody's gonna laugh at that. You got to pay the people off. I try to take those moments and make them into situations."

But after so many years and so much success, it was inevitable that he'd start to think he could simply tell anecdotes without adding all the twists. The audience, now conditioned to Cosby's style, indeed seemed to laugh at some pretty slim material from time to time, just enjoying Bill's company. *The Tonight Show* proved that.

The album was "dedicated to all of the kids who *were* kids and are now big kids that remember the fun they had when they were little kids because little kids have more fun than big kids because they forget pain a lot quicker than big kids."

It was a weak record. And after seven years, audiences were getting itchy. When Cosby did a long, drawn-out routine on how he and his friends used to go to the theater and watch Buck Jones movies, it was predictable, nostalgic rambling. Some critics always thought anybody could stand up and tell embellished childhood anecdotes and get laughs. But not anybody, even Cosby, could get away with simple unadorned anecdotes.

At this point in Cosby's career, overexposure, familiarity, and a depletion in his supply of "our gang" stories seemed to have combined to lessen the appeal of his kid stuff. There was something else, too—a revolution in stand-up comedy.

At the start of the sixties, Cosby had sailed in as part of the fresh new wave of comedians, the "wholesome" ones taking over from Sahl, Bruce, Berman, and Winters. But now the cycle had come around, and, at its center, was the ghost of Lenny Bruce. The Bruce revival was on, ignited by the stage and movie versions of *Lenny*. And riding in on the wave was a dirty-word parodist, George Carlin. Other hip comics appeared too, like Cheech & Chong, whose albums began to easily outdistance Cosby's in sales.

If childhood humor was, for the moment, on the way out, what else could Cos do? He'd bombed with a two-record set of Las Vegas routines, but maybe it was because it *was* two records, and on the ill-fated Tetragrammaton label. Cosby vowed to try again. Besides, if he was making fifty thousand dollars a week entertaining the well-heeled Vegas crowd, maybe some of those heels would pay for a new record of his adult material.

Cosby followed up the weak *When I Was a Kid* album with the exact opposite, *For Adults Only*, complete with a smirking cover shot of naughty Mr. Bill.

Bill had done mildly risqué humor once in a while—a bit on a silly gorilla too stupid to mate and an anecdote about him and Robert Culp in Spain, looking for Spanish fly, only to be asked by a cab driver: "You American? You have any . . . American fly?"

Now he was ready to give the audience "the filth show." Besides, he was born, he said, in "Filthadelphia."

He talked about his hotel room: "They've got a mirror over my bed. I swear . . . I was uneasy going to sleep. When I sleep I toss and turn and when I woke up I thought I saw a naked skydiver coming at me. . . .

"But I don't know what it's there for. I really don't. You gonna shave in bed? What the hell you gonna watch? All I know is from the way I . . . ummmurrr, you get a broken neck tryin' to watch . . . and Camille's a virgin Catholic, I know she ain't peekin'!"

One of the best bits was a hilarious verbal cartoon about the time Bill's two young daughters, totally ignorant of the facts of life, snuck into the bathroom and watched him stand in front of the toilet "doing God's work." They begin to squeal, "Oooooh, Daddy, you got a Wallie Wallie!" And the next thing he knows, they're standing there, wetting the floor all over, trying to imitate him.

Some fans were disturbed by Cosby's vaguely blue material, and his new emphasis on husband-wife and parent-versus-child material. This was a painful transition period for Cos, and many didn't understand where he was headed. He was almost starting over, now that he was developing a new slant for his old style.

Today it's obvious that a forty-eight-year-old man would look silly, if not perverted, doing nothing but routines about what it's like to be a little kid fighting grown-ups. Today Bill primarily goes the other way, but does impersonations from the kids' point of view too, and has retained *some* childlike qualities of fun. But back then, it was a tough time. And Cosby's "blue" couldn't match Carlin's, or that of the old master, Lenny Bruce.

The album got a push from his nervous record company, with a full-page ad in the new, nasty humor mag, *National Lampoon.* Cosby's album was shown tied up in a brown paper wrapper and addressed to "George Whiteman" with the tag: "Amazing phonograph record brings renewed happiness to thousands of married couples . . . by one of the world's leading authorities on marriage and domestic affairs."

The new image didn't work too well. A restless Bill Cosby told writer Muriel Davidson, "I'm only thirty-four years old. My time is *now.* If it isn't now, it may be never. And I can't afford 'never.' I never could."

Cosby embarked on a flurry of new activity that became a frenzy, till it almost seemed to exhaust Bill—and suddenly exhaust the patience of columnists and writers. They started to turn on him and his one-man media blitz. Suddenly the word for Cos wasn't *cool* or *cute.* It was *Arrogant,* with a capital *A.*

Chapter
13

Nineteen seventy-two. Cosby had a bunch of record albums in the racks and *Man and Boy* in the theaters. He was also touring the country with his nightclub act, working on his master's degree from the University of Massachusetts, and appearing with a painted face, in an educational TV special called "Prejudice," to talk about bigotry and ethnic slurs. He was making jazz albums. And, when three CBS vice presidents, Fred Silverman, Perry Lafferty, and Irwin Segelstein, out-hustled ABC and visited Cosby's Amherst home, they came away with a contract for a new Bill Cosby show called . . . *The New Bill Cosby Show*. And they were also prepared to star Cosby in his first made-for-TV movie.

At a press conference, a female reporter said, "But Bill, my readers think you're spreading yourself too thin."

Cosby stared at her for a moment and said, "Madam, I just don't care what your readers think, see?"

When he began to talk about all the projects he was into, the reporters turned off. When he let show some of the Cosby drive, and talked about his plans and ambitions, the reporters turned on him. This Bill Cosby was arrogant, self-centered, and even rude. What hostility!

Cosby simply was not going to listen to negative thinking or tolerate it. He wasn't going to be told what he could or couldn't do. Too much was at stake. He had his own production company to keep afloat, he had to navigate a change in comedy style, he had to correct slumping record sales, he had to pursue his movie career, he had a family needing his attention, and the demands of a dozen or more charity organizations. And he was going to teach a course in broadcasting at USC. Too big and just plain too busy to coddle the press, he alienated them severely with his talk of his goals, his philosophy, and his ambitions. But they were not going to interfere with his plans.

It didn't seem that anybody could. But an exception was Robert Culp, who visited Cosby with a script one day. Bobby, according to most observers, was having a rough time. Now he was hoping to get a break with a new movie, something called *Hickey and Boggs*. If Bill Cosby became Hickey, maybe the movie would get off the ground. Cosby was completing negotiations for his first TV movie, but stopped everything to help Bobby. Cos felt he owed him one.

As it turned out, there was still a certain amount of reluctance from the major studios. *I Spy* was a dinosaur, and many had forgotten about Culp and Cosby. Besides, Culp wanted to direct the movie himself, and Cosby was still unproven at the box office.

Fortunately, Fouad Said, a director of photography from the *I Spy* show had made millions from the creation of the Cinemobile, a van that could transport sets from place to place. He was ready to support the duo. The script, rewritten slightly for Cosby, was provided by a promising newcomer, Walter Hill. He was only ten years away from becoming famous as the writer of Eddie Murphy's *48 Hrs.*

Behind the scenes, the men renewed their friendship, and Culp assessed the change in Bill. "When he came in to read for *I Spy,* he was scared and angry. Angry because he realized what could be, what *was,* at stake. He has the fastest, sharpest, most flexible mind of any man, white or black, I know. Bill is a loner. The only way he has changed since our days together is those hangers-on. They're gone."

For the film, Cos and Culp rejected their superhero stances and played a pair of luckless private eyes, relics from the bygone Raymond Chandler era. They end up involved in a battle between mobsters, a Chicano street gang, and the police. The booty is $400,000 in stolen bank loot.

Along the way they grumble about their domestic problems (both are divorced), find themselves the targets of a helicopter attack, and end up in gunfights all over Los Angeles, including Dodger Stadium. In one scene, they take refuge behind a Rolls Royce Silver Cloud, which gets pumped full of bullets.

Working on a very tight budget, they managed to get a used model and hoped to repair the damage and re-sell the car after it and the scene was shot. But, according to Culp, there was a perplexing mystery involving the car that even Hickey and Boggs couldn't solve: It was impounded by the Treasury Department.

"They tore it to pieces, ripping every bit of the upholstery off. They found what they were looking for—two pounds of heroin, about two million dollars' worth—hidden in the frame. . . . We were used by someone. Of course, it is possible that somebody made a terrible mistake. We may never know."

Reviewers who did manage to catch the modestly budgeted flick before it flickered out of neighborhood theaters didn't seem impressed one way or the other. *The New York Times* found the duo "a good deal less convincing" as private eyes than they had been as spies. "As anti-heroes, both Mr. Culp and Mr. Cosby are serious, sullen and extremely laconic. Terse passes at dialogue merely indicate their personal relationships and their concomitant, bloody, thankless mission. . . . Understatement is obviously the keynote here but *Hickey and Boggs* still owes us a fuller explanation despite all the chasing and carnage."

Culp tried to explain that he was celebrating a pair of "classic super-losers in a losing profession, managing to pull it off one last time because of their devotion to each other."

Now Cosby could devote himself to his CBS deal. Cos hadn't liked one aspect of it—having to live in Hollywood while doing the variety show. He had to agree, though, that it would be cheaper to do the show there, and was told that some of the money saved would be used to make the show better. Cos reluctantly went "bicoastal," with homes in Amherst and Pacific Palisades.

Robert Wood, CBS's president at the time, told reporters: "Bill Cosby has a total commitment to education. Fortunately for us, he realizes that television offers an ideal medium for narrowing the gap between education and entertainment."

Before the premiere of the variety show, or the new *Fat Albert and the Cosby Kids* cartoon series, there was the CBS movie. Filmed in Norwalk, Connecticut, and broadcast on February 25, 1972, Cosby's return to TV was in *To All My Friends on Shore.*

He played Blue, a family man with a mission. Driving a cab all day, he saves his tips in a secret hiding place, hoping for the day when he will have enough money to buy his dream house. He takes on extra jobs, works tirelessly for his cause, and sacrifices "today" for "tomorrow." He hardly has time for his wife Serena (Gloria Foster) or son Vandy (Dennis Hines). "I'm losing the man I love to a rotten old house," the woman complains.

Things change when Vandy becomes ill. He's diagnosed as having sickle-cell anemia, and it's fatal. For his dying son, Blue explains that there are yesterday people, today people, and tomorrow people. The past is for yesterday people. Blue has always been dreaming of tomorrow. But now all that matters is today.

What would make the boy's days happy? "I just want you," Vandy tells his Dad. They begin to share the few todays that are left. It is on a boat ride together that Vandy is given the job of pilot. And it is there that Blue tells him, "Say goodbye to all your friends on shore."

The basic story was written by Cosby himself. The screenplay was by Allan Sloane, who received an Emmy for his work. Cos also wrote the musical score for the film, which was praised by *The New York Times* as "a warm, sympathetic, sentimental portrait . . . quietly appealing. Many of the family-life details are good. And the central performances are excellent."

Cos now began work on his variety show and on the cartoon show *Fat Albert*. He brought with him a renewed sense of purpose and dedication. "People don't want Mr. Nice Guy," he fumed. "They want Archie Bunker. A lovable bigot." Cos was determined to do something about that.

In the spring, Cosby received his master's degree, but vowed that he would continue onward, to his doctorate. And as the premiere date, September 1972, approached, he gave his writers on the new variety show a taste of school discipline.

"If they write something very good," he said, "I shake their hand and tell them so. I grade their work the same as I would a school paper. Some get A's, some D-minuses."

Some people behind the scenes were not happy with Cosby's highly disciplined approach and his fierce determination to produce something worthy at all costs. In a way, it seemed incongruous. After all, this particular project was supposed to be one of those light, funny variety shows, with sketches and songs.

Hindsight shows that something else was out of place—the whole idea of doing a variety show in 1972. At the time, this type of entertainment was dying. The old *Hollywood Palace* and *Ed Sullivan*–type programs were defunct. Just the year before, the host/dance routines/songs/comedy skits format had killed shows starring Glen Campbell, Johnny Cash, Don Knotts, Tom Jones, Jim Nabors, Tim Conway, Lawrence Welk, and Andy Williams. Tastes had changed. People couldn't agree on musical tastes, and comedy sketches were, with the exception of *The Carol Burnett Show,* now in its fifth season, a dull exercise.

Cosby and CBS drove headlong into disaster. Scheduled at ten P.M.

Monday nights, they were going to lose all the little kids who couldn't stay up to watch. Leading into the show at nine P.M. were the wheezing *Here's Lucy* and the limping *Doris Day Show.* The slim family audiences that did bother to sit through the sitcoms were dead snoring by ten P.M., or so numbed by cuteness they needed to switch to ABC for some football violence with Howard Cosell.

With ABC football to the right of him, and *The NBC Monday Night Movie* to the left, Cosby charged ahead with his premiere show.

On the program, he was interrupted almost before he could begin by Foster Brooks, the "lovable lush" with the white beard parted in the middle. Brooks played a gaseously drunk CBS executive welcoming him to the network and at the same time humorously wrecking the show. Stumbling in from "my burnt mattress in the alley," the exec welcomed Bill to CBS, which stood for "Cocktails, Believability, and Sausage."

Sidney Poitier and Harry Belafonte were the guests. Keeping up with the times, one of their sketches with Cosby utilized racial humor. Racial comedy was once again a hot topic in comedy, thanks to *All in the Family, The Flip Wilson Show,* and *Sanford and Son.* As a militant, Harry Belafonte tried to convert Cosby to his cause. "Come home, black brother!" Bill looks at him. "To Philadelphia?"

In another scene, Foster Brooks goes over some CBS memos with Cos. "I hope you looked at your contract," he says, "because at the end of the year you have to marry Carol Burnett."

With undistinguished sketches and songs, there was sometimes more entertainment behind the cameras than in front of them. One day Flip Wilson came by during rehearsal. The "enemy" from NBC snuck onto the stage at CBS's Studio 41, drew a toy pistol from his pocket, and suddenly made a grab for one of the script girls.

"I'm taking hostages!" Flip shouted. "I'm gonna hijack this studio to NBC!"

He got a mild smile out of Cosby, who was having an uneasy time supervising the writing and directing of the show, *and* keeping up with his many other projects as well.

Cosby's amiable smile wasn't in evidence quite as much as it had once been. To the press, he sometimes lost patience with the traditional dumb questions about his career, his wife, his kids, and his race. As he tried to put his series on the right track, his sense of purpose was viewed as "arrogance." With his reputation on the line, some around him couldn't understand why he wasn't simply his TV image—silly and constantly smiling.

When he flew up to Vegas for a gig, audiences were astonished by Cosby's actions. Cos, the man who knew that you must never break in front of an audience and show anything but a nice guy in control, lost control.

A stagehand was sawing wood backstage, and the noise became more and more audible. Cosby's smiling, comic mask fell away as he stopped his act, put down the microphone, and suddenly stormed backstage through the swirling curtains.

A few minutes later the sound of sawing ceased. The confused audience waited. Finally Cosby pushed back through the curtains. Gone were the easy, laid-back ad-libs, or even the good-natured show of mock anger one might've expected.

He talked for a few more minutes, then said, "Good night." The audience just sat there in disbelief. The show was only halfway through, and suddenly it was over.

A similar incident had occurred nearly a decade before to Shelley Berman. A phone rang backstage, he showed his irritation at losing his concentration, and was forever more branded as a petulant, hyperstrung loon. After ten years of building up his image of affability and tolerance, Cosby was nevertheless beginning to take the rap most comedians face. Why wasn't he funny twenty-four hours a day, and always smiling? In Cosby's case the intensity, the striving for perfection, and his own rising star began to reduce his tolerance for minor annoyances from people or things.

Insiders wondered how long it would take for Cosby to start fighting with his co-producer on *The New Bill Cosby Show,* George Schlatter. Schlatter had a reputation for being a difficult, dominating personality. He'd guided *Rowan and Martin's Laugh-In* to the top, but left the show in a bitter war over its direction. Bill Bohnert, set designer for the new Cosby show, noticed immediately that "they both had a different viewpoint on humor. Bill liked very long, sort of gentle stories building to a smile, and George wanted one-liners."

George and Cos could argue about almost anything. From the beginning, Schlatter was adamant about the set designer he planned to hire. Cosby felt a loyalty to the set designer he worked with on *The Electric Company,* a man he knew to be quick and efficient. The two men tussled for quite a while before they stopped and realized they were both talking about the same guy—Bill Bohnert!

On some points, the two men did agree. Schlatter was more than willing to hire more blacks on Cosby's suggestion. "This was still very early on in television, when there were not very many blacks involved," notes Bohnert. "I do know that Bill was instrumental in getting a black cameraman and a black stage manager. These were big steps forward at the time."

Cosby's physical appearance reflected his impatience with the slow struggle for equality. For 1972, Cos was sporting a kind of *Soul Train/ Mod Squad* look, with bushy hair that might have been considered a conservative Afro. He wore long sideburns, a mustache, and a thumb-sized black liberation flag in his lapel. Schlatter insisted the mustache had to go. "When you spend weeks growing a mustache," Cos reflected wistfully, "you almost fall in love with it. I had a good, big, thick mustache. Everything you drink with it, you drink twice. But Schlatter felt it covered too much of my face. I took the sideburns off as well. He said something like, 'Gee whiz, I think it would be groovy if people could see your face.' "

They didn't see it for long.

If there was any consolation for the demise of Bill's variety show, it was that he wasn't alone. Julie Andrews, the movie superstar lured at last to do her own variety show, suffered the same ignominious fate.

The happiest thing about the ill-fated series was that it gave Cos the chance to meet with some of his Hollywood friends and even put them on the show. Of the comedians, Cos had a special fondness for Groucho Marx, and it was mutual. Groucho said to Charlotte Chandler, "Have you ever seen Cosby in a nightclub? He's fantastic. He doesn't tell any jokes. He does impressions of people. Like how a mother will talk to her child, and how a father will talk to the same child. Things like that. . . . He's brilliant, this man."

Chandler taped some of the informal get-togethers between Cos and Groucho in 1972–73, and they appear in her book on Groucho, *Hello I Must Be Going*. They showed the mutual respect and love of fun the two shared, singing old songs with wacko titles—from an a cappella version of "The Darktown Strutters' Ball" to "You May Look Like a Hawaiian, but You're Just Another Nigger to Me."

When Groucho received his Academy Award, Bill was at the party with him, along with other table guests Jack Nicholson and Marvin Hamlisch. Later, after appraising the Oscar, the only major award Cos hasn't won, Cos said, "Now, you take this gold streaker . . . he looks like one of my people as opposed to one of yours. Got some nice buns.

And a great profile. I could see a woman at home getting quite horny over that, and going out in search of it."

Groucho was fun. So was Cos. But nice fun wasn't where prime-time TV was going. Referring to the short-lived *Jimmy Stewart Show,* Cosby mentioned, "Jimmy Stewart went down the drain the same as I did playing Mr. Nice Guy."

It looked like Cos was out of touch, too mild in an era when Flip Wilson was jiving it up as Geraldine and Richard Pryor was beginning to hurl racial epithets at both whites and blacks. But the children were still there. Cosby's other TV project proved to be a rewarding success on all levels.

The idea of a cartoon show based on the "Cosby Kids" had been in the works for a long time, but at last *Fat Albert and the Cosby Kids* was slated for a Saturday-morning spot. With that program, Cosby was fighting a battle against mindless junk TV, violent superheroes and in- anities like *Scooby Doo, Motormouse,* and *The Brady Kids* cartoon show.

"The way I see the show," Cosby told journalist Cecil Smith, "it will be so casual in its teaching, the children will never know they're being taught. It will have Fat Albert and old Weird Harold and those other characters I made up, but they will get themselves involved in things like mathematical equations and what geometry is all about and why."

If the show was educational for kids, it was, in a way, an education for Cosby, too. Dr. Dwight Allen at the University of Massachusetts had arranged to make the show part of Cosby's studies. He'd be earning college credit, turning in the scripts almost as though they were term papers, working with the professors on evaluating the techniques Cosby was using for combining education and entertainment.

Once more the critics were skeptical—until they saw the finished product. *TV Guide* would proclaim it "perhaps the best cartoon pro- gram on television, and the most thoughtfully presented. . . . Cosby presents the cartoon material (in live action introductions) acting as a parent or adult friend. He makes the transition for the child from the real to the fantasy world, much in the same way a parent or grandpar- ent says, 'Now I'm going to tell you a story.' He reappears during the show to explain the actions, define words, and point out a moral."

"This is Bill Cosby comin' at you with music and fun. And if you're not careful, you might learn somethin' before it's done." With simple introductions like that, Cos became a Saturday-morning pal.

Like most cartoons made for TV, the animation wasn't much and the shows tended to be "amusing" rather than "funny," but the series maintained its standards through more than ninety half-hour episodes.

The cast included a youthful version of Cosby, his squeaky-voiced brother Russell, and three of the oddest kids ever seen: Fat Albert, a sort of a benign Muhammad Ali, who spoke softly and in rhyme most of the time (after falling down and creating a giant hole, he says, "Hey, hey, hey, made my own subway"); Dumb Donald, whose strange, loose stocking cap fell halfway down his face with just his eyes showing through, as though the cap were somebody's underwear; and Mush Mouth, who talked with sputtery extra *b*s. ("Are you kidding?" would come out "Ah be-you be-kibbeding?" About the only name he could possibly have pronounced right would've been B'nai B'rith.)

Some episodes were overtly "message" oriented. In one, Fat Albert and the gang play hooky to go skateboarding, play in the junkyard, have fun. Then they meet two bums and learn that the "easy life" means bum food, sleazy surroundings, and no friends. After all, if you can't read or write, how can you even get a letter from your pal?

Suitably chastened, Fat Albert comes to school the next day two hours early. "Ever hear of drop-outs?" he asks. "Hey, hey, hey, we're drop-ins."

After the cartoon, Cos offers a few more words on the subject. "School may not be the greatest," he admits, "but the worst thing in the world is not going to school when there *is* school."

Then Albert and the gang sing a song about the coolness of school. To those who play hooky they sing, "You think you're the smart guy, just 'cause you stayed away/ If you're so smart, well, think real hard: Tell me, what did you learn today?"

The show was a learning experience for Bill's own children. Young Ennis was a faithful *Fat Albert* watcher for years. When he was eight, the little boy received a treat. He was brought into the recording studio to watch a *Fat Albert* soundtrack being recorded. He stared wide-eyed at the imposing array of tape recorders and mikes, and the technicians doing their jobs.

When Cos came to the microphone and started to read from his script, the little boy was awestruck.

"Dad," Ennis whispered in surprise, *"you're* Fat Albert?"

Many episodes of the show were drawn from Bill's monologues, such as the classic one about him and his brother having their tonsils taken out. In cartoon format, a black doctor with a Transylvanian accent frightens the boys. They tell their parents, "We can't go. Tell the doctor we can't go. We're too sick to go to the hospital!"

When they're forced to go, the boys gather their gang around to hear "our last will and tenement" and dolefully hand out all their "good junk," like decoder rings and kazoos, knowing they are about to die.

The hospital stay has moments of comic misery, too.

"My neck itches," Russell whines.

"Why don't you scratch it?" asks Bill.

Russell responds, "It itches on the *inside!*"

That particular show offered a lesson of a different kind. It showed to what lengths Cosby and his crew would go in order to be absolutely truthful and instructional. Someone asked if it was such good advice to tell the viewing kiddies that a tonsillectomy doesn't hurt. And what about ice cream? In Cosby's monologues and in the script, he had said, "The best part is you can eat all the ice cream you want." Well, was that true? And was that such a good idea considering the calories involved?

The show's producers contacted the assistant dean at UCLA, Gordon L. Berry, and put the question to him. He in turn put the question before a panel of teachers and professors for approval. The panel could not reach a decision because one of their members, a professor in the UCLA psychiatry department, was out of town, and his viewpoint was vital. Production waited while a pediatrician was consulted. The pediatrician pointed out that not *every* child can eat ice cream anyway, because some kids are allergic to it. The question was tossed back to Dr. Berry, with the suggestion that a few more doctors and nutritionists be brought in. This was *in addition* to Dr. Berry's CBS- and Cosby-approved panel of anthropologists, psychiatrists, sociologists, and specialists in children's education.

In the end, the simple joke about ice cream was left in, as well as the sight gags of Fat Albert and the gang crashing into the hospital corridor in search of the room where Russell and Bill were having their ice cream feast. Cosby did turn up at the end of the show to admit, "Having their tonsils out *did* hurt . . . but they'll be over it soon." The gang sings: "Don't be scared of a hospital . . . you'll get good care at a hospital . . . you'll be repaired at a hospital."

The *Fat Albert* series covered a lot of different subjects. As if to vindicate once more Bill Cosby's profound point of view on racial equality, a study conducted by CBS confirmed that Cosby's approach— treating blacks and whites as people first and stereotypes dead last—was paying unexpected dividends.

Polling a sample of black and white kids, CBS found that only twenty-nine percent even mentioned that Fat Albert and his gang were black. When asked to describe the show, and how the characters were like or different from themselves, less than a third even thought to answer that there was a racial difference. This was remarkable, especially since the show *did* have an all-black cast, had some realistic lower-income locales, and even injected a few childish racial jokes now and then (Fat Albert, seeing that Weird Harold keeps his spare change in his shoe, says, "Hey, hey, hey, you're a real *sole* brother").

Cos devoted much of his time to the *Fat Albert* cartoons and to his studies at his Amherst home. He still played stand-up gigs, even in his hometown, though he felt Philadelphia was never quite as strong for him as other cities.

He loved going back to Philly to meet with friends from high school and Temple, and sometimes he'd even go back to the old neighborhood to surprise the new crew of kids there. Once he and a group of fans got into a stickball game on a sidestreet. There wasn't much room to stretch out. The buildings on either side were foul territory and a ball bouncing off the far wall in back would carom back so quickly that nobody could get more than a double out of it.

So Bill got up at bat, studying the situation carefully. The street stickball veteran took an uppercut swing and popped the ball straight up, about six stories in the air. Cos took off like mad, loped around the "bases" (touched the wall, stomped on the sewer lid, then around to the Buick) and home. Home run before the ball came down.

That's how you play the game, kids.

Meanwhile, Cosby tried to break in with the real big boys. Cos bought into the Golden State Warriors basketball team. "It's more a sentimental gesture for me," he said. "The team originated in Philadelphia and that's where I'm from. I just bought a percentage of the team for old times' sake. It's not really any big deal."

As for his own career, Cosby cast a bitter look at the new television scene. Of *All in the Family* and its comical bigot Archie Bunker, he said, "Some watch the show and love Archie because they think he's right. . . . Names like kike, nigger, and the rest of them never seem to die." Even now he maintains a smoldering dislike for the show. On a 1985 Phil Donahue broadcast, he reiterated, "My opinion is that the man never apologized for anything. He had a wife who said, you shouldn't say that, and a son-in-law who said, you shouldn't say that, and a daughter who said, you shouldn't say that. But the man himself became a hero to too many Americans for his shortsightedness, his tunnel vision. And I'm really a believer that that show never taught or tried to teach anybody anything."

Cosby coupled his TV show with a new album, *Inside the Mind of Bill Cosby,* but it wasn't a big seller. Reluctantly he had to admit that "the market is saturated with Bill Cosby" albums, and they weren't moving.

Cosby had released one jazz instrumental album on Uni. For Sussex, he released one more, with exactly the same title as the first, which may have been an act more of stubbornness than prudence. After all, the title *Bill Cosy Presents Badfoot Brown and the Bunions Bradford Funeral Marching Band* was a tongue twister.

The album notes showed Bill's irritation with critics and seemed to underline that he was rehearsing for retirement. After disclaiming the record as something "fun" and not to be taken "seriously," he wrote, "I wish the critics reviewing this album to know thusly. It is no big thing, until I notify you of such. . . . No matter how small the fans of the Bunions Bradford album, if they can purchase enough, the next album shall follow. If they don't, the Bunions Band is playing its own funeral march."

Another problem with Cosby's instrumental albums, aside from testy album notes, were the notes within. They were jams, ten- and fifteen-minute cuts mostly. Part of the joy and feeling of a jam is being there, preferably playing an instrument. A musician can delight in riffing for fifteen minutes because *he's* doing it. It doesn't always translate on cold vinyl.

Cosby's success on cold vinyl had gotten pretty cold. As for making more movies, he was leery of all the "blaxploitation" films now on the market. "Give them some sex, some guns, and some cocaine to capture the black audience," he said, describing the movie moguls' thinking. "It is a proven formula, man. Maybe they will throw you a *Sounder,* but in the end it is easier to throw some dude $500,000 and tell him to give with the sex, tits, and coke."

When he did agree to an infrequent interview, he complained about past interviews. He remembered how Earl Wilson sat around his hotel room ordering floppy deli sandwiches and asking incoherent questions with his mouth full. He remembered others who were drunk. He remembered being used to liven up other people's articles and make them look good with his jokes. And he recalled Rex Reed misquoting him, sticking in soul phrases he'd never uttered. Cos figured that Rex must've confused him with Godfrey Cambridge. It was Godfrey who punctuated his speech with "hey, baby" this and "hey, baby" that.

More and more, Cosby felt that the direction to go in was education and children's programming. His *Fat Albert* cartoons won him the Children's Theater Association Seal of Excellence. His studies at the University of Massachusetts were progressing far better than his variety show was, and once more, there were rumors of retirement. If Cosby had definitely lost ground in prime-time television and in record sales, maybe retirement *was* the answer. It was something for Cos to think about as he spent time at his Amherst retreat with his wife and children.

Chapter

14

" I thought kids were the simplest little creatures in the world, once upon a time.
That was before I had any of my own. But me, I'm someone who likes
to do things in the overkill method. I had a kid—my wife helped, of
course—and then another and another . . . and well, you get the picture, don't you?"

It seemed there were so many Cosby kids there weren't enough days
for them to arrive on. Bill and Camille's fourth child, Ensa Camille,
arrived on April 8, 1973, the same birthday as their daughter Erika.

A month later, Cos had a gift for other parents—a prime-time cartoon special, "Weird Harold." In it, Cos and his pals, including the
Weird One, put together go-carts and have one of the wildest, most
violent races in the history of childhood. After the carnage, the kids end
up before a judge, handcuffed by cops. But all ends well: The kids are
allowed to race again, under adult supervision. The story was based on
monologues from Cosby's *Wonderfulness* album, recorded nearly a decade earlier.

Actually, Cos had found quite a different sport to occupy his attention during this slack period in his career. He was developing into an
excellent tennis player and had begun making the rounds at celebrity
tournaments across the country.

He took the short trip down from his Amherst home to compete in
the Robert F. Kennedy Memorial Tournament in New York, in August
1973. At the benefit for minority children, Cos demonstrated both his
tennis form and his comic form.

With the crowd watching, Cosby defended himself against the awesome serving power of Stan Smith. He braced himself defiantly. But just
as Stan tossed the ball up, Cos comically fell apart, the racket flying out

of his hands, his legs flapping back and forth in shuddery terror, his face a mask of eye-popping fright.

Smith dropped the ball and doubled over, wandering away from the court in laughter as the crowd roared.

Later on, Cosby was back again, in a weird mixed-doubles match. He was paired with Alan King, and the sight of the two cigar-chomping comics wearing equally oversized tennis hats was bizarre enough. But playing opposite them was the most mixed male-female doubles opposition anybody could face: Bobby Riggs in drag. Wearing a bonnet and an old-fashioned red-checked dress with puffy lace sleeves, Riggs baffled Cos and King completely, and even when Riggs threw a bunch of chairs all over his side of the court, making it an obstacle course, the two comics couldn't solve his lobs and spins.

But Cosby got the last laugh. In the midst of play, Riggs lost control of his dress, and the top slipped down. Cos immediately ordered the game forfeited on account of this braless breach of tennis-court etiquette.

"This is probably the first sport I've entered where I really feel like trying to achieve my full potential," Cosby enthused.

In those days, he had plenty of time to practice his game. Cos still went out on the road for his stand-up engagements, but was more interested in watching his three daughters and son grow up.

Television audiences didn't see Cosby trying to compete with the new trend—the racial comedy riots of *All in the Family, Sanford and Son,* or *The Jeffersons.* Instead he appeared between the shows, in his commercials for a variety of products.

Even in this, he was a trailblazer, although some have trouble finding redeeming value in commercial interruptions. Before Cosby, it was rare to see a black in an ad. The few blacks who did appear usually pitched some product with an ethnic slant, like Southern fried chicken. But Cosby would become the spokesman for products and companies that symbolized America: Coke, Ford cars, Texas Instruments calculators, Jell-O. It proved that Cosby was very special indeed, one of the very few stars who could be appreciated—if not loved—by all of America. Big corporations and big advertising agencies don't take risks that could offend potential buyers. Cos proved to be the perfect choice.

Meanwhile Cosby continued to work on his studies at the University of Massachusetts and involve himself in educational projects. He visited inmates at the Pennsylvania State Prison and made a film for kids of the ghetto, called *A Date at Graterford.*

In it, Cos talked about the road to prison—beginning with street gangs and petty crimes. He interviewed many inmates, including one who was in jail for a senseless murder committed during a gang fight.

Now, the inmate reflected, "One of the things that I've always felt I needed in my life were people who understood me, so I feel that maybe a lot of the problems the young children or the young adolescents are encountering can be possibly overcome, or some solutions can be found if they can just sit down and talk with somebody."

Cosby's face was sober. He said, "You had to kill someone and be laid away almost for life before you found you're an intelligent human being."

Some wondered when Cosby would do another movie for theatrical release. "I don't do blaxploitation pictures," Cos said. "I prefer doing things I can feel good about."

Out on the Coast, several actors were trying to feel better about Hollywood's product. Paul Newman, Barbra Streisand, Steve McQueen, Dustin Hoffman, and Sidney Poitier banded together to form First Artists, a company that would give the stars the same creative control over their projects that Charles Chaplin, D. W. Griffith, Mary Pickford, and Douglas Fairbanks had when they started United Artists fifty-four years earlier.

Poitier was hoping to begin filming a series of family pictures featuring blacks. In the past few years, it seemed that every black in a movie was either a superdetective or superpimp. Cosby was eager to join in the project, and with Harry Belafonte joining as well, Poitier had a film with blockbuster possibilities, the first black "superstar" movie.

With these big stars, Poitier received financing, and more than 1,300 blacks won jobs on the project, behind the cameras as well as in front of them. Filming for the movie, *Uptown Saturday Night,* went without a hitch.

As time for the premiere approached, everything was looking good. It seemed that nothing could stop the movie from becoming a triumph. Just to add icing to the cake, Cosby went into the studio to cut some promotional radio commercials for the film.

Cos had so much confidence in his ad-libbing, he didn't want to overrehearse. That could kill his easy brand of humor and make the commercial sound phony. The Muhammad Ali of comedians, Cos sometimes treads the fine line between confidence and cockiness. He often uses just enough of his skills to thrill audiences with a performance that could, if he weren't a consummate showman, meander into coasting. Somehow, after giving away a few rounds with ringside chatter and audience jokes, he always comes back with knockout punchlines.

This was his knockout commercial:

"Hi, this is Bill Cosby. Remember the good old days when you used to go uptown to Harlem and have a good time before it became very dangerous? Well, you can still go uptown without getting your head beat in by going downtown to see *Uptown Saturday Night.*

"This way the people are all on the screen and won't jump off and clean your head out. Bill Cosby, Sidney Poitier, Harry Belafonte, starring in *Uptown Saturday Night.* This is PG, Parental Guidance. I thank you."

The ad went over so well that, after it had aired on July 3 on a few New York radio stations, it was reviewed in the local papers.

BILL COSBY INSULTS HARLEMITES, roared the New York *Amsterdam News,* the city's powerful black paper.

Some black leaders demanded to know how white radio stations WINS, WABC, and WCBS-FM could dare run such an ad. Then they learned that black stations like WBLS-FM and WWRL had run it too.

Seizing on the Bill Cosby slur, the manager of the Apollo Theater fired some bullets to go with the bombshell controversy. "Why should blacks have to go downtown to see a movie about themselves?" demanded Bobby Schiffman. He had been furious long before July 3. On June 16, when the movie had its sneak premiere for the press, he distributed ten thousand cards reading, "Wonder why uptowners can't see it uptown now? Because Jim Crow lives; 125th Street is still the back of the bus, moviewise that is." Even though the press party was held in Harlem, at Vincent's Pub on 125th Street, Schiffman was still angry.

Once again strides forward toward pride and dignity were met with resentful sniping and conflict. And there was Bill Cosby, stuck ankle-deep in the mire of his admirable ad-lib ability.

If both black and white radio stations were guilty, then there was no scapegoat. If every film company's policy was to give first-run films to expensive downtown movie houses before uptown and neighborhood theaters, then there was no scapegoat. The press soon ignored the radio stations and Warner Bros. and went after Bill Cosby.

Along the way, they grabbed Melville Tucker, the film's producer, and demanded to know if he was *with* Cosby and *against* them. "Being perfectly objective," Tucker said, "I can see where some people in Harlem might feel some resistance to [Cosby's] statement."

Cos was in Europe at the time. When the storm raced over the Atlantic, he took no shelter. He didn't ad-lib his answer, he sent a carefully worded telegram instead:

"I wrote the 'blurb' with the intent that it be humorous. Like lots of things humorous, sometimes a person has a lapse of taste. I retract it. I take back everything said and am sorry for any harm done. I apologize to the Harlem community and to black communities in all other cities. Had I listened to it after having done it, I'm certain I would have wiped it out myself."

For a decade Cosby had been working hard to present the right image, and he had worked hard on the project, proud to join with Poitier and Belafonte to produce an important film that was for blacks without being "blaxploitation." The sting of the mistake was hard to take, and the anger that met his joke—the fury of being turned against for a quip —gave him a feeling of bitterness, even betrayal. Cosby had always known how easily audiences could turn and how fickle fans could be.

The next time Bill picked up the papers, he was expecting more bad news. In the *Los Angeles Times,* he read that *Uptown Saturday Night* was "one of the year's most enjoyable movies, the old-fashioned kind that leaves you feeling good all over." *The New York Times* called the performances "marvelously funny . . . Mr. Cosby is particularly good. . . . [The film is] so full of good humor . . . such high spirits that it reduces movie criticism to the status of a most nonessential craft."

Cosby, Poitier, and Belafonte had themselves a coast-to-coast hit.

The film was, in a way, beyond criticism. Viewed ten years after, it's very mild fare, but at the time it was designed to be a likable film, a film to get people together, a family film with some positive black images. Its goals far outweighed any complaints over the actual amount of laughs, or Poitier's ability to direct comedy.

In fact, the film is more an action-adventure epic with some humor thrown in. It follows a factory worker (Poitier) and his good-time pal (Cosby in a porcupinish mustache-and-beard set) in a mix-up with gangsters.

At first, the comedy stems from the very straight, unfunky Poitier's attempts to spout earthy dialogue. "You know something?" he tells his wife. "After twenty years, two kids, and four jobs—you still got the biggest butt I ever saw." A viewer would have to conclude from the view supplied that he hasn't seen many.

Cosby also is given exaggerated black dialogue that sounds strange.

Coaxing Poitier to come with him and visit Madame Zenobia's after-hours parlor, he smiles broadly and says, "They be some fiiiine mamas comin' in that place!"

At the dice table, Cos is all fey smiles, checking out the foxes and the galloping dominoes. The hostess roars, "If you can't stand the heat, stay out of the kitchen. Harry Truman, 1952." Cosby answers, "I remember. I was in the kitchen when he said it."

The fun and games end when gangsters break in and rob the joint. It's a menacing moment, and for Poitier and Cosby it means the loss of their winnings—and the lottery ticket in Sidney's wallet that turns out to be worth $50,000.

The two men hit the street trying to track down the gangsters. Under Poitier's leisurely direction, the men take time out to visit church. Flip Wilson has a tiny, jokeless sermon to give on loose lips: "The looser the lips are, the faster the ships sink. And some of the lips in this congregation could sink aircraft carriers." Richard Pryor has a cameo too, doing his frightened, trapped-mouse act. He plays a faint-hearted private eye with eye trouble. "See my right eye? See how bloodshot it is? That's from sleepin' with one eye open." Then he whines that the "supernig-ger" detectives in the movies get the drop on whites and crooked cops, and romance women, and "I ain't had a woman in *months!*"

Cosby actually gets to drop the comedy completely in one unusual scene. He enters a bar and lectures, "I am off the corner! I get mean when you mess with my green!" Not only does he pick a fight with a very tough-looking patron, he even punches him out. When Poitier attempts a similar feat, complete with insults ("You're so ugly it's against the law in twenty states to marry you!"), he nearly gets his head handed to him.

Eventually they meet up with Harry Belafonte, who parodies Marlon Brando's godfather with puffed cheeks and a raspier-than-usual voice. Flanked by his gang, he informs the duo, "We gonna beat the black off both of ya." And if he doesn't, rival gangster Calvin Lockhart will.

Caught between the warring gangs, Poitier and Cosby get involved in high-speed chases and some tense moments of kidnap and near execution before the movie ends with tears of joy mixed with the laughter.

The film was uneven, symptomatic of black movies at the time. Poitier and his crew were still trying to find themselves, caught between mass market and down-home funk, between ethnic humor and playing it straight, between comedy and adventure. For Cosby, the film marked his first full-fledged movie success, even if he did it in hirsute camou-

Cos and his dreamago-cart, on his third comedy special, an April Fool's Day treat back in 1970. *(Courtesy Movie Still Archives)*

Backstage waiting for friend Sammy Davis, Jr., to finish his show, Bill's flanked by the two most important women of his life: his mom Anna and his wife Camille. April, 1970. *(Courtesy Frank Edwards/Fotos International)*

Mike Douglas and Bill Cosby duet on *The Mike Douglas Show* in 1973. Who's the better singer? Well, Douglas hit #6 with "Men in My Little Girl's Life." But Dr. Cos scored a #4 with "Little Ole' Man: Uptight-Everything's Alright." *(Courtesy Movie Still Archives)*

Below left: Monday Night Football tackled Temple's most famous halfback, but before *The New Bill Cosby Show* kicked off, Cos and Peter Sellers got together to play with the prop man's beard and moustache collection. *(Courtesy Movie Still Archives)*

Right: Cos pauses in the middle of the road: a November, 1975 comedy-variety special costarred him with country singer Loretta Lynn. *(Courtesy Waring Abbott/Photo Trends)*

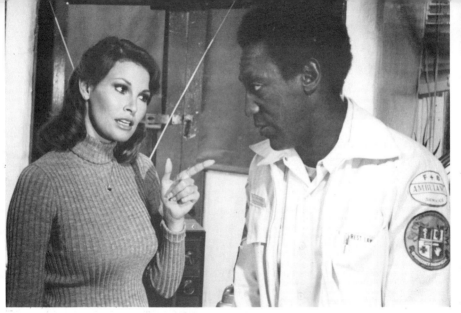

"Don't call me 'Jugs,'" warned Raquel Welch in 1976's *Mother, Jugs and Speed*. Bill's name in the movie was no better—"Mother Tucker"—and the picture came and went with speed. *(Courtesy Movie Still Archives)*

Cos and Denise Nicholas shared *A Piece of the Action* in 1977. "It's a nice clean relationship," Bill said of the two film characters. "They discover each other and like what they've found." *(Courtesy Movie Still Archives)*

November 23, 1977. Camille and Bill
are floored: Bill Cosby has gotten
another honor, his star in the sidewalk
of Hollywood's Walk of Fame. *(Courtesy
Frank Edwards/Fotos International)*

Sporting a trademark skyscraper stogie:
Cos sits back and watches some tennis
after serving up laughs during the 7th
Annual R.F.K. Pro-Celebrity Tennis
Tournament in the summer of '78.
(Courtesy Ron Galella)

The blameless grin of childhood was part of Bill's routine on the comedy special, *Bill Cosby, Himself.* *(Courtesy Movie Still Archives)*

Feelin' great at forty-eight: Cos has TV's #1 show, makes ten million dollars a year, and can come home to the wife he adores and five kids who have all turned out just right. *(Courtesy Movie Still Archives)*

The Cosby Show premiered with (top row, left to right) Tempestt Bledsoe, Malcolm Jamal Warner, Lisa Bonet, along with Bill, Phylicia Ayers-Allen as his wife, and little Keshia Knight Pulliam. Sabrina LeBeauf (not in photo) joined the show soon after as the Huxtables' fourth daughter. *(Courtesy Movie Still Archives)*

Above left: Between scenes on *The Cosby Show*, Cos took the mike and told the studio audience his series would maintain high standards. Copycat shows fumbled with Cosby's family formula but failed. *Newsweek* called Flip Wilson's show "a dull thud," *Here's the Mayor* a "dog," and *Growing Pains* simply "icky." *(Courtesy Ronald L. Smith)*

Above right: Skeptical Cos and tired Malcolm wait out a technical delay announced by stage manager Gary Vinson. Cos made headlines during the show's second season for putting an "Abolish Apartheid" sign on his TV son's bedroom door. *(Courtesy Ronald L. Smith)*

Below: A rare look at *The Cosby Show* set. For Cos it's a short walk from the living room to the kitchen: Phylicia Ayers-Allen, Keshia Knight Pulliam, Bill, and just between the stage manager and the cameraman, Tempestt Bledsoe. *(Courtesy Ronald L. Smith)*

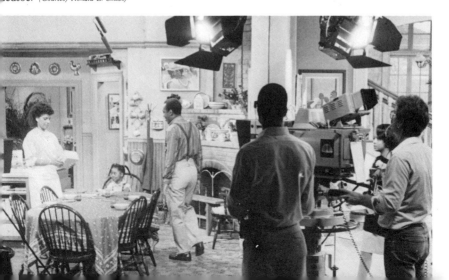

Bill and Keishia Knight Pulliam have a father-daughter relationship off camera as well as on. *(Courtesy Movie Still Archives)*

A special night out for Bill and Camille. The Cosbys spend most of their private time at their home in Massachusetts and shun show business socializing. *(Courtesy Ron Galella)*

flage. The film may have added to his image among more militant blacks, who could appreciate his "new look" and dialogue that was closer to the street.

The presence of Pryor and Cosby together, early on, showed the difference in their performing styles. Pryor was funny with his woeful, frightened expressions, his knitted brows. He was the perfect victim. Cosby had more dignity and sympathy. The scenes where he and Poitier were frightened (Poitier did quite a bit of eye-popping) didn't work. Cosby simply doesn't have fright comedy in his repertoire. Impersonating a child, in a comedy monologue, yes. But playing an adult? Definitely not.

In stand-up and in comedy records, Pryor was becoming the superstar. In 1973, Cosby's swansong album for MCA, a record of Fat Albert childhood comedy, lost out at the Grammy Awards to Cheech & Chong. Now, in 1974, there was no record label for Bill Cosby, and the Grammy went to *That Nigger's Crazy*, by Richard Pryor. In fact, Pryor would end up with three Grammies in a row.

Out along the concert route, Bill was still strong with the Vegas crowd, but his appearances elsewhere sometimes proved disappointing. At the 3,200-seat Nanuet Theater-Go-Round in New Jersey, Cosby barely drew twenty-five-percent attendance. He took it pretty well, demonstrating that the relaxed, rested Bill Cosby of 1974 was far different from the harried workaholic lecturing columnists and crew members on his film, record, and TV projects in 1972.

"I had some opening remarks like 'I'm glad to be here,' but that was before I saw the crowd! Is there a flu epidemic? Is this a Jewish holiday or something? Are the stores open late? Give me some sort of an out!"

Now, at the movies, Cosby was suddenly a better draw. Sidney Poitier recalled, "The success of *Uptown Saturday Night* told me that black people wanted to laugh at themselves and have fun. They were weary of being represented on the local movie screen by pimps, hustlers, prostitutes, private detectives, violence, macho men, and dirty words. They wanted to have good, clean, family-type fun."

Family fun and sports fun seemed to be the answer for Cosby. Into 1975, Cos kept up his vow not to bother with records, and to avoid TV. With the arrival of another daughter, Evin Harrah, he had a full house: Erika, Erinne, Ennis, Ensa and Evin. The *E*s, he always said, referred to "excellence."

Cosby was setting the example, pursuing physical and mental excellence. He was working on his doctoral dissertation, entitled "An Integration of the Visual Media Via *Fat Albert and the Cosby Kids* into the Elementary School Curriculum as a Teaching Aid and Vehicle to Achieve Increased Learning." He wanted "to show my children that, although their father does one thing, it's possible to do many things."

Cos also published a book, *Bill Cosby's Personal Guide to Tennis Power, or Don't Lower the Lob, Raise the Net.* It's filled with pointers on improving tennis skills, and also some stern warnings: "If you and the ball happen to arrive at the same place at the same time . . . body spasms will not help you execute the stroke!"

The same competitive spirit Cosby brought to Temple University could now be seen on the tennis court. In one memorable pro-celebrity charity match, tennis trainer Alexander Scott faced his old friend, tennis pro Kelly Robinson. It was an *I Spy* reunion that brought the crowds to their feet.

In the mixed-doubles event, Cosby was teamed with Fred Stolle, and Robert Culp was joined by Arthur Ashe. Cos dazzled the crowd by winning several heated exchanges with Ashe, and charmed them with a little clowning in between matches.

Cos later teamed up with Elliott Gould, Dean Martin, Jr., and others to play basketball in an exhibition to help Sugar Ray Robinson's Youth Foundation. But their opposition was members of the Los Angeles Rams football team, and they were blown away by a thirty-point margin.

At home, Bill was still getting blown away by the simple things in life. Like teaching kids how to keep their ice cream on the cone. Cos surprised some visitors by insisting on picking up a fallen scoop of ice cream, rinsing it off, and putting it back on a daughter's cone. "Have you bought ice cream lately? Do you know the price of ice cream?" he asked. The Cosby kids learned not to waste food, and even to watch out for sloppy eating where the ice cream dribbles down the sides of the mouth: "Each dribble's worth maybe three cents!"

Cosby made his lone major television appearance of 1975 in November, starring in a Monday-night special, "Cos: The Bill Cosby Comedy Hour." It was a coasting special, closer in concept to the failed variety show of 1972 than to the Emmy Award winning monologues he did on earlier specials. The guests were mainstream performers that had no flair for Cosbyan comedy: Tony Randall and Karen Valentine. And the supporting music was supplied by country star Loretta Lynn. Despite some help from such veteran writers as Alen Robin and Art Buchwald, *Variety* spoke for most critics in reporting that "this was a disappointing use of an extremely ingratiating performer. . . . The scissors-and-paste production was flat."

It just seemed to confirm that movies were the way to go. Agreeing with him was tennis partner and friend Sidney Poitier.

Chapter
15

With the success of *Uptown Saturday Night,* Poitier and Cosby said, *Let's Do It Again,* and that film was even more of a triumph than the first. When it arrived in 1976, TV shows like *Sanford and Son, Good Times,* and *The Jeffersons* had covered most phases of the "new black comedy" style. With nothing more to prove, Poitier and Cosby could strike a relaxed balance between overtly ethnic, funky material and general jests, without having to answer to either black or white extremists.

"Sidney's looser," Harry Belafonte said, dropping by the set one day. A $2.6 million budget contributed to Poitier's confidence. For the first film Cosby basically had worked for a percentage of the gross and $75,000 up front. In order to appease Poitier and stay with the movie throughout its long shooting schedule, Cosby even suspended nightclub gigs that could have been worth, in his estimate, $500,000.

The superstar cast assembled for *Let's Do It Again* included the distinguished actor Ossie Davis and two hot TV personalities, Jimmie Walker and John Amos. Again, Cos plays a feisty kind of guy, picking a fight with somebody far heavier and taller.

"Watch your lips or they may get you into something your behind can't get you out of!" he shouts. But when push leads to fight, he decides to forgive the man. After all, it happens to be George Foreman, in a cameo role.

Poitier wisely stayed the straight man, leaving Cosby more room and time to play around. In a very Cosbyan scene, Cos pulls a little girl onto his lap, only to find she's wet his leg. "She's all finished now," he announces, giving the moppet back to her mother. When he eyes a hot-looking lady in the parking lot, he smiles at her—forgetting that his pants are wet and that he looks like some kind of perverted bum.

Cosby and Poitier belong to a mystic lodge that wants to build a day-care center. So he and Sidney concoct a scheme: Take the lodge's money, gamble it in New Orleans, and earn enough to make the dream come true.

The guys bring their wives to New Orleans with them, mixing business with pleasure. In the pursuit of pleasure, Cosby speaks the most R-rated dialogue of his film career. At dinner in a fancy restaurant, his wife (Denise Nicholas) kisses him on the cheek, thanking him for the vacation.

"Is that all I'm gonna get?" he asks.

"That's all you're gonna get in public."

"I'm gonna lay a blockbuster on you tonight," he teases.

"Yeah? Well, I have a block for you to bust, baby, so you better bring a whole lotta hammer!"

"Have hammer . . . will travel," Cos enunciates coolly, "and go deep . . . into . . . your crevice!"

This shocks Poitier's wife. How can they act so blue (or, perhaps, too funkily black) in public? But in *Let's Do It Again* the relaxed attitude lets people be what they are. When the woman wonders aloud "what people would say" if they heard such coarseness, Denise answers, "They would say I was having a horny conversation with a man . . . and he was pickin' up on my thighs! Are you gonna sit there and say Clyde ain't been hittin' your switch regular?"

"We don't let the whole world know about it," the woman huffs.

"No," Poitier agrees, "we whisper a lot!"

Cos and Poitier find a scrawny fighter (Jimmie Walker) from Possum's Paw, Alabama, and hypnotize him into thinking he can defeat the champ. When the scam works, they must stay one step ahead of the furious bookies. The plot twists in and out, as they must keep hypnotizing and unhypnotizing the two fighters.

It was a pleasing film on all counts. Con man Cos proved here that he could easily have assumed some of the slick, lovable, comic-hero roles given to actors like George Segal or Burt Reynolds. The movie broke box-office records when it opened at the Criterion Theater, achieving a three-day gross of $64,000.

Even the New York premiere, with money going to Harlem's YMCA and YWCA, reflected the relaxed attitudes of the times. Once Steve Allen made a joke to a black audience, "It's so nice to see blacks, Negroes, and Afro-Americans all living together in harmony." Here, there was proof that some of the division in the black community, between militancy, Afro-Americanism, mainstream, and down-home funk, could be overcome. That night, John Amos showed up in a dashiki and cap. Poitier and Cosby wore their business suits. And Jimmie Walker turned up in flashy threads with a blonde on his arm. Three very different points of view, but all seemingly acceptable that night.

Praise for Cos was lavish. The *Christian Science Monitor* wrote, "Cosby shows flashes of pure genius." The *Village Voice* loved "the free-wheeling jiving, put-down artistry" he showed. His success in the two hip Poitier films proved he could be a big star in films.

Next, for his first "mainstream" movie (discounting the quickly made and quickly forgotten *Hickey and Boggs*), Cosby shared star billing with the female superstar of the era, Raquel Welch. The movie was a hard, hip, *M*A*S*H*-style comedy, *Mother, Jugs and Speed.*

The two Poitier films had been funky, cool black comedies. Here Cosby was cast in a ferocious, hip "black comedy" of semi-sick humor. Cos plays Mother Tucker, an ambulance driver and medic who works for a sleazy company run by scuzzy Allen Garfield.

"Times are tough," Garfield lectures his crew, "the country's goin' to hell. You take inflation, welfare, recession . . . there's nothin' we can do about that. But thanks to mugging, malnutrition, assassination, and disease, we got a chance to make a buck!"

The grimly humorous ambulance calls include: a lady wrestler thrown out of the ring and doused with soda by jeering fans, a giant black woman who has fallen off a chair while changing a light bulb, and an overdosed hippie stretched out in his underpants.

Their problems are treated with cruel humor. The wrestler is propositioned by ambulance driver Larry Hagman, playing a guy with necrophiliac proclivities toward any dead or unconscious woman. The black woman is strapped to a gurney and ultimately hurtled out a window, down a fire escape, and into the path of an oncoming truck. The overdosed kid is nearly taken away by the cops until Cosby rushes in with a paper, calling, "That's our stiff! Read 'em and weep!"

In a devilish moment, Cos drives along mumbling, "Oh! Why did the Lord tempt me this way?" A bunch of nuns are daintily crossing the street, single file. He jams on the siren and rides right into them as they break into a panic-stricken run for cover. Cos chuckles in amusement as he flies by.

Raquel Welch initially plays a thankless "Hotlips Hoolihan" role. Everybody calls her "Jugs," even Cosby. Eventually she's allowed to go out on calls. Cos makes Raquel handle the problem of a loathsome fatty who's caught himself in his pants zipper. As she grimaces, trying to free him, Cos grins and says, "She has the dedication of a jungle mercenary." Then it's off on more cases, some with peculiar in-jokes ("Mrs. Natasha Gurdin got her hand caught in a garbage disposal," one call goes, referring to Natalie Wood's real name).

Cos, dubbing himself the "Brown Hornet," has fun with his job—most of the time. One case involves a strung-out junkie who pleads with one of Cosby's partners, "I need drugs. Morphine, Demerol, whatever you got." It's Toni Basil, about seven years away from rock stardom. Just to prove she's frustrated, she takes out a rifle and blows the medic away.

Back at the office, grisly Larry Hagman has a pool going, betting on how many corpses come in each day. He's bet on eight for today. With Cosby's dead partner, it would be nine. "He doesn't count," Hagman protests; he's not really a paying customer. Cosby smiles, comes forward, and suddenly attacks Hagman, pummeling him to pieces, sending him crashing to the floor.

Cosby is unquestionably the star of the movie, handling the comic high points, and having all the no-nonsense authority to take charge during dramatic shoot-outs and punch-outs. His performance indicated that he could enjoy a full movie career, playing everything from tough private eyes to the kind of seriocomic roles Elliott Gould, the star of the movie M*A*S*H, seemed to be getting.

But the movie's jumble of sadistic comedy, violence, and pathos put critics off-balance. The Los Angeles Times praised Cosby's "strong, coherent performance" in a film that they felt should be awarded "a tarnished cup for shrill sludgery." Time praised Cosby's "affectless cool." But just to show that ethnic digs would forever pop up even in totally nonracial films like this, Andrew Sarris of the Village Voice limply labeled Raquel Welch "pure plastic" but then attacked Cosby for doing "a Stepin Fetchit imitation."

The film had some success as a cult item, enough so that, when M*A*S*H ended up a tremendous TV hit, Mother, Juggs and Speed also became a TV show. In 1978 a pilot episode was screened by Variety. Although a g was added to Jugs to appease feminists, nothing of value was added. "The cool, relaxed presence of Bill Cosby" was missed, and, worst of all, the actress playing Raquel Welch's part didn't fill it to its full potential: "Her breasts are exiguous compared to the ones flaunted by the robust Raquel."

For Cosby, 1976 was not just the year of his renewed movie career. He also made headlines for achieving one of his most coveted goals in private life. It would give him lasting pride—and give detractors fuel for some of the nastiest sniping of his career.

Chapter
16

I t was a picture-perfect May afternoon in the country. Camille wore a softly shirred pastel dress that touched the ground and a wide-brimmed picture hat, neatly tied with a bow around her conservative neckline. She was the very model of elegance, recalling the Gay Nineties in demure sweetness. Her mother-in-law was in "Sunday best" too. But the hero of the hour was Bill Cosby, in mortarboard cap and gown.

With a smile and a handshake, Bill stood before University of Massachusetts Chancellor Randolph Bromery and accepted his degree, doctor of education. From now on: *Dr.* William H. Cosby, Jr.

"Mom just went crazy today," said Bill with pride. "She used to say 'Education's a must.' If she was dead, she would have gotten up to come here today. Her tears mean so much."

The man with the degree was also a man with a renewed purpose. In just three months, in fall 1976, he was going to show off his commitment to education in entertainment with *Cos*, a new variety series. Who better than Dr. Cosby to teach kids and make them laugh at the same time?

But was this the right time?

The warning signs were up and the lines were drawn. The time between eight P.M. and nine P.M. had been ruled "Family Hour" in an attempt to curb the networks' tendencies toward shows with violent heroes and violently jiggling heroines. For this first hour of prime-time, G-rated entertainment *only!*

What happened was disaster. Shows stuck in the eight-to-nine- P.M. time slot were wishy-washy failures that quickly dripped down the drain. Without .38-caliber guns and 38-D bras, "family" shows came and went: *Swiss Family Robinson, The Captain and Tenille, The Tony*

Orlando and Dawn Rainbow Hour, Holmes and Yo Yo, The San Pedro Beach Bums, Young Dan'l Boone. High morals? Yes. And low ratings.

With such a high mortality rate, who would dare try to entertain without sex or violence? What star would risk professional disaster for a cause?

Dr. Bill Cosby.

The educator, the star of *The Electric Company* and *Fat Albert,* the father of five, he would champion a family show that didn't take on racism, abortion, vasectomy, crime, or other Norman Lear-y topics.

The doctor theorized, "The Family Hour has to do with something very, very technical. It has to do with using the tube to address itself to educational values, to teaching, to subjects that have to do with morals." If that didn't sound entertaining, the doctor assured critics that his show would not "be turned into a university instead of a variety. This hour will be funny without preaching and teaching."

Just to make it even more of a challenge, ABC put Cosby up against the only praiseworthy family show on TV, *The Wonderful World of Disney,* and the blockbuster *60 Minutes.* Cosby's steely determination never wavered. He vowed to be "more inventive" in finding ways to reach the family audience.

Kay Gardella was, for over a decade, the kindest, most supportive columnist in Cosby's corner, a woman who plugged virtually every Cosby special, TV show, and movie. But even she cautiously questioned his heroic charge into TV's wasteland: "Of late Cosby . . . gives the impression he's carrying the burden of responsibility for all the young people of the world on his shoulders. It's a good thing somebody does, I know, but it tends to inject a little of the preacher into the comedian. Dangerous inflation of opinion can result, and must be guarded against."

Cosby's admirable vision was tunnel vision, and it led him down a long, bottomless shaft. His one chance was that folks would be in the mood for something funny. *Disney* and *60 Minutes* weren't funny. But neither was he.

The simple TV show *Cos* produced a simple reaction from critics: diabetic shock. They cringed when he did an Art Linkletter bit, interviewing little moppets for forced humor. They fumed at wholesomely boring guest stars like Cindy Williams and Bruce Jenner, and snored through the music of Chicago, a band most any age group could tolerate, but few really could get excited over. There was a roving cast of "bright young players" and some animation, and, in the middle of it, Bill Cosby and his monologues.

Variety called the show "an uneven mixture of clever and silly material . . . deliberately tailored for tots' brief attention spans." There wasn't enough of pure Bill Cosby. *TV Guide*'s Cleveland Amory had less tolerance and reflected the long-knifed attack *Cos* was getting around the country: "Cosby comes on the way he does in those commercials in which he persuades little children to eat their canned peas. Sixty seconds of Cosby being cutesy-poo in a commercial is one thing; sixty minutes of the same every Sunday night is another."

Amory was among the critics who trashed Cosby's newly won doctorate: "With Cosby's new Ph.D. in education . . . perhaps he feels he has a professional obligation to be boring. . . . Bring back *Lassie*. At least that show admitted that it was a dog."

Frustrated by the show's problems, Cos turned up at a party at the Playboy mansion in Los Angeles to relax. One of the guests was Tommy Smothers. Tommy and Bill, both purveyors of childlike comedy, were not buddies. Rivalry among comics is not unheard of, and neither is mutual coolness, if not resentment. Tommy walked over to Cos, smiled, blinked up at Bill with his one blue eye and one green one, and began talking.

Nobody seems to recall what was said. All they remember is the sight of Tommy Smothers sprawled on the floor from a sudden right-hand lead from Cosby.

The crowd was hushed. Tommy was an athlete in his own right, a gymnast capable of some picture-perfect push-ups and handstands, but he was no match for Cosby. One punch was the proof.

Later, the swollen-cheeked comic claimed that he was only trying to compliment Bill on his new TV show. The last words Tommy heard were "You've been asking for it."

What would happen the next time he happened to run into Cos? Smothers said, "I guess I'll have to hit him again—with my face."

A close business associate of both Bill and Tommy, who noted that both men could be moody at times, recalls, "I don't know what the specific reason was, but they never really liked each other. Tommy can be really strange. Tommy must've been juiced or whacked, 'cause Cosby certainly wasn't. And Tommy must've said something that pissed him off. Tommy is very physical. And Bill can be very physical. I can easily see the two of them punching the shit out of each other."

Fans who heard about the incident were shocked. Even intimates were surprised. Most people who have seen Bill angry say that his rage takes the form of "smoldering," and that the look in his eyes and the grim-set jaw is enough to send people walking briskly in the opposite direction.

Meanwhile, Cosby continued to take a beating in the newspapers, and the heat was directed not only at *Cos* the show, but at Cosby the man.

Cosby had always seemed "too good to be true," and now was the perfect time to attack him for his "goody-goody" TV show. Perhaps the cycle was turning again and people were tired of his particular style and personality. Maybe, with the violent success of Richard Pryor, there was some backlash against Cos for remaining a mainstream "Tom" performer à la Sammy Davis.

Cosby wasn't helping the cause; like a parent, he lectured columnists who didn't understand his vision. And his conservative viewpoints seemed out of touch with the times. Guys like Pryor were putting on the toughest of street-jive dialects, while Cosby took a dim view of Black English: "We're lighting a fire that has no use, a fire that doesn't warm anybody, where you're going to make up your own language, your own mathematics and sciences. That's just an easy way out. We need black people in space and science programs and in many other areas. While these hoodlum packs are out roaming the streets and saying, 'What it is, is what it is' and 'Right on' and giving handshakes and challenging each other over a piece of cement that the *city* owns, there are some very bright ones . . . who could contribute something to society."

On another passionate subject of the times, interracial sex, Cosby was on record as a moderate. "Many white chicks feel they'll get soul if they ball a black man they don't even care about," he'd told *Playboy,* "and the black goes to the white because of the white's status in this society; the black person is supposed to *gain* from making love to a white. And the white is giving up status. . . . If a white chick is with a black guy, she's saying, 'Look at me, look at what I'm giving up, look how I'm going against society. Man, am I brave.'

"Now, I'm not talking about love, just balling. . . . I've been with white cats who've looked at black chicks I wouldn't be seen with anywhere and heard them say, 'Man, she is fantastic-looking.' . . . I'm talking about whites who have a desire to make love to a black . . . [to] dig that African or extra blackness that says this person is 100 percent black."

Typical of the prickly heat he was getting lately was this from the

Village Voice: "Cosby has become unfunny in recent years, a monotonous young fogey capitalizing wherever he can on his splendiferous teacher thing . . . clubby-kissing the ruling-class hand of Johnny Carson, making spokesman commercials for such established heels as White Owl cigars, and Pan American airlines. He has evolved into a kind of self-parodying sap."

Okay, the liberal press was shifting to more militant black entertainers. And youngsters, like those who outgrew *Mad* magazine and bought *National Lampoon* and jeered *Mad* for not growing with them, were resenting Cos for playing Daddy for a new generation. And maybe gentle comedy was out of favor for some people. Surely *somebody* had some kind words for "Cos"?

Well, the Black Writers' Caucus didn't. When Bill began *I Spy,* there was no such thing. Now, a decade after Bill's breakthrough, the group singled out Bill Cosby—because Bill Cosby was being *unfair to blacks.*

"We don't feel anyone owes anyone anything," chairman Jim Tisdale told the newspapers, "but we felt it would be only fair or rational that a show with a black principal would be represented with blacks in all creative, craft, and technical areas." Sure, Cos may have done a couple of good things and broken a lot of ground for the race, but only two of the twelve writers on this show were black.

The Black Writers' Caucus vowed to set up pickets outside the studio and show Bill Cosby a thing or two.

"I'm really on my countdown to retirement," Cosby said in the midst of all this. "My first series, *I Spy,* ran three years. *The Bill Cosby Show* lasted two years. My first variety hour lasted one year. And this show? If I'm lucky, it will run thirteen weeks."

Try a lucky seven weeks. Trick or treat: On Halloween, "*Cos*" became one of the season's earliest casualties. He'd given them sweet treats—but it looked like viewers wanted nasty tricks.

For months critics had been giving Cosby a piece of their minds. Now, for peace of mind, he spent the Christmas season at home in Amherst. Camille told *Essence* magazine, "It's like what you read about in books. There's snow, sleigh rides, tobogganing and sledding. We roast chestnuts and marshmallows in our fireplace."

Their formal Christmas dinner, for twenty people, featured homemade bread, two different main courses (meat and fish), and three types of desserts. Eubie Blake played the piano and told stories.

At that beautiful time of year, Cosby had the satisfaction not only of time with his family, but of remembering, by the contrast of those dire years in the Philly projects, how much he'd been blessed. It was unfortunate that, to judge by the failure of *Cos,* some of the old-fashioned sentiment, love, and humor he knew was gone from many American TV screens. And not even missed.

Chapter
17

Cosby may have been criticized in 1976 for not being like the new comedy sensation, Richard Pryor, but at least one person came to his defense. A reporter came up to Pryor and began to compliment him, saying, "Richard Pryor's humor is not cute like Bill Cosby's was or is." Pryor snapped, "Bill Cosby's one of the funniest men in the world, and I don't like being compared in those terms. Saying Bill Cosby is cute, that is offensive to me. Bill Cosby is not cute, he is one of the funniest men in the world." He once admitted, "Bill Cosby paved the way for Richard Pryor," even though Pryor's first TV exposure, on *The Merv Griffin Show* in 1965, wasn't long after Cosby's TV arrival.

On TV, about the only avenue open to Cos was the usual one, *The Tonight Show*. But as if to add fuel to Cosby's growing negative image among critics, talent coordinator Craig Tennis reported that Cos was mercurial in temperament, veering from cordiality to rudeness for no apparent reason. Of course anxiety on *The Tonight Show* was always high when a guy like Cosby was around, because he disliked heavy rehearsal and planning, and preferred winging it—always dangerous.

Tennis recalled having "both very good and bad experiences . . . Bill changes from moment to moment—you never know where you stand with him. I've seen him come on *The Tonight Show* completely unprepared and yet work himself into a monologue that is warm, original, and killingly funny. At other times he's been cold and aloof, maddeningly playing the superstar, and even talking down to the audience."

It was through the *Tonight Show* appearances that most fans saw the gradual change in Cosby's monologue style over the years: He changed from an impish, childlike performer to a more adult figure, coming out in a vested suit, walking his special stately walk, and enunciating through the cigar flaunted between his teeth.

Now that the mainstream TV audience had eroded for Cos, he looked elsewhere for support, and found it in one of the most unlikely places: R&B music. Spurred by the success he was enjoying from the Poitier films, Cos shifted into comedy funk on record, signing with Capitol and releasing an album called *Bill Cosby Is Not Himself These Days, Rat Own, Rat Own, Rat Own.* He certainly wasn't himself, except in one way—he was, as usual, taking a bold step and doing it largely on instinct.

What really made Cos think he could succeed with an R&B record anyway? He hadn't made *any* record in three years, hadn't really had a successful record in five years, and had had *no* success with a musical album in more than a decade. And he was aiming at a very slim target. Back in '76, rock and soul fans weren't known for having any sense of humor when it came to lampoons of their idols.

His first single made the charts: "Yes, Yes, Yes," a parody of Barry White's school of butterfat balladeering. With a female chorus cooing "yes yes yes" over and over, the deep, intimate vocal oozes words . . . of love?

"I wowna ask ya a question, darlin' . . . last night baby . . . did you go through my pockets?"

The song turns out to be a ballad about the miseries of married life, and a chick who wrecks the car, cheats, and drives her man nuts. On similar cuts, Cos lampoons gooey R&B love songs with such observations as "My love is so deep for you, you can't find it" and "I picked a brick up and waited for you . . . wanting to smack you dead upside the head . . . yes, I've been in love . . . and you can have it!"

The other tune making the charts was "I Luv Myself Better Than I Luv Myself," a James Brown rave-up with Cos crying, "Good God! Feeling Good! Good God! Yow!" before trying to quack and bark out his soulful joy.

Cosby followed up this success with his first new album of monologues, *My Father Confused Me, What Must I Do?*, a beautiful comeback album blending contemporary humor and stories about parents and children. He lampooned pot smokers unable to handle simple reality, even seeing a hamburger grilled and eaten. Wide-eyed and frantic, Cos cries, "The dude took a piece of round meat! And threw it on the grill! Then he turned it over! It had black stripes on it! I said far out! And the dude *ate it!* I can't deal with it!"

He drew a bizarre picture of his runny-nosed daughter whose shimmering face made her look like "The Glazed Donut Monster." Given a rest for several years, his childhood routines sounded fresh and more vibrant than ever. In one he talked about his mother's clichés of violence, like "I will knock your brains out." That one really frightened young Cos:

"That's horrible, man. She's gonna hit you in the head and your brains are gonna fall out on the floor! I always wonder what would've happened if I went to the store, got some calves' brains, and when she hit me threw 'em on the floor . . . pow! Knowin' my mother she'd say, *'Pick* those brains up and *put* them back in your head and *don't let* your brains fall out of your head again! Or I will knock you into the middle of next week!'

"Please do, 'cause I'm having a rough time this week."

Cosby proved to be closer to his old, amiable image—even when pressed by pushy reporters. One time he was appearing in a celebrity tennis tournament and refused to grant individual interviews to the press. A reporter—from *Interview* yet—who used the byline Tinkerbelle, disregarded the ban and came up to Cos anyway. Cos actually invited the reporter's company, and answered some very precocious questions.

Tinkerbelle asked if Cos went "to Temple . . . the college, I mean, not the synagogue." Cos answered, "Both. It's fifty-five-percent Jewish." Tinkerbelle quizzed him on another vital matter: "You get propositioned much, Bill? You must. How do you deal with it?" Cos answered, "I just tell the guy to go to hell."

Cos enjoyed himself on the tennis court—and he would soon be named by *Tennis* magazine as the top male celebrity star in the country. He was also having fun at home with his five kids. He had fun the day he dropped by the Sotheby Parke-Bernet gallery in New York and bid on a painting of a black child and his Sunday school teacher done by Thomas Hart Benton. He got it. He only had to pay $105,000.

He had commitments to various causes that cared about him as much as he cared about them. He was a member or active on the advisory boards of the Mary Homes College, Ebony Showcase Theater, the Black Film Foundation, Workshop for Careers in the Arts, the Communications Council of Howard University, the Smithsonian Institution, Institute for Creative and Production Studies in Radio and Television, the American Sickle Cell Foundation and the Studio Watts Workshop. Among others.

Looking over his shoulder, he saw Richard Pryor test the Family Hour with his own variety series. Cosby's show hadn't lasted past October 31, 1976. Hey, Richard's show was off the air by October 20, 1977. There may have been some slim satisfaction in that, but Cosby was his usual temperate self in commenting on the problems of network TV:

"I've got nothing to offer in a series," he said. "I don't know how to get lucky with them when you've got fifteen writers sitting around throwing paper airplanes and handing you stuff to rewrite and try to make good. That's why I was glad to see Pryor pull out because they eat you alive.

"I've done so much people can't box me in," Cos added. He kept juggling the club dates, records, *Tonight Show* gigs, TV commercials, and movie roles. He was even in the news again when, after he had received his master's and Ph.D., Temple University belatedly gave him his bachelor's degree. Also, he had a new film coming out with Sidney Poitier, *A Piece of the Action.*

"What the picture touches on," Poitier told reporters at the time, "is the question of young people who are underprivileged, unemployable, or unemployed in major cities." The story also dealt with the punishment of crime, because "our system is punitive rather than rehabilitative. . . . I believe our system of justice helps create criminals."

In the story, Poitier and cat burglar Cos have Robin Hoodish intentions of taking money from those who are taking from the poor, but end up rehabilitating themselves and thirty kids, with the help of a retired policeman played by James Earl Jones. They naturally have to battle corruption and bad guys along the way—with Cos in a derring-do highlight leaping from a twelve-floor office building to safety.

Cos found "something very new and different" in his expanded romantic role opposite Denise Nicholas, who had played his wife in *Let's Do It Again.* Here she and Bill had a chance to flesh out the relationship. She played the coordinator at a community center who has no idea his occupation is slightly larcenous until they get to know each other much better. "It's a nice clean relationship," Bill said. "They discover each other and like what they've found."

Shooting was low-key, and, when the crew went on location to Chicago, they would sometimes find Cos passing the time with neighborhood winos, joking and rapping. The film was more warmly emotional than the first two, and *Newsweek* applauded: "It touches the funny bone and the heart and leaves you feeling good. This is by all means superstars Poitier and Cosby's best effort."

When the returns came in, though, the film had failed to generate quite the response at the box office that the two previous Poitier-Cosby movies had. Cos was disappointed. He liked the film because it had less "foolishness" and more of a story. Poitier was tired out: "*A Piece of the Action* was my own original idea. I then had to work for many months with the scriptwriter. And then I had to make the picture, direct it, and act in it, and once it was finished, I had to edit it, oversee the scoring and all the manifold details attendant on getting a picture out. . . . I have to rest my bones, restore my juices. You will not see another movie of mine until two years from now."

Cos put out a few more records for Capitol, both music and comedy. They broke little new ground, though in keeping with the style of the seventies, Cos was covering territory he couldn't have covered in earlier childhood remembrances. Like wet dreams:

"First time it happened, I got scared. I didn't know what it was. I said uh-oh, I ate too much cornbread last night. . . . I rolled up the sheets and went down to the laundromat, five in the morning, did my own sheets. Nine twelve-year-olds down there doin' their sheets too, man. After that I'd get out of school, three-thirty, four o'clock I was back in bed again: Come on, whatever it was! Yes indeed, three glasses of water and a picture of Dorothy Dandridge and I was on my way."

There was talk of Cos starring in another black superstar film, *The Wiz,* playing the Tin Man. Other commitments prevailed, but it might've been cute if Cos had played the wizard, and the original songs were kept. Then Dorothy and her friends could sing, "We're off to see the wizard, the wonderful Wizard of Oz. We hear he is a whiz of a wiz, if ever a wiz there was. . . . Be Cos, be Cos, be Cos, be Cos, be Cos . . ."

The new year brought a different movie, *California Suite.* It proved that the name Bill Cosby meant big box office. After all, he was sharing billing with people like Jane Fonda, Maggie Smith, Michael Caine, and Walter Matthau.

Neil Simon's idea was to present four stories about guests at a Beverly Hills hotel. The subject was relationships in crisis situations, in situations of need, love, and support. Two episodes were heavy; the other two, starring Matthau and Cosby, were the slapstick-filled comic relief. The trouble was that neither the director, the writer, nor the stars were especially noted for slapstick.

Now over forty, Cosby was slowing down, developing into a cigar-in-mouth stoic, a vaguely scowling parent humorously disturbed by the brain-damaged antics of his children. Nearly sixty, Matthau had perfected his taciturn, grumpy persona.

Matthau bristled at director Herbert Ross. "Herbie wanted me to pull out all the stops, to be outrageous," he fumed. "I said that I liked myself better when I speak very quietly." His segment was an artistic embarrassment, an overdone slapstick farce in which he made inane faces, wrung his hands, and popped his eyes over the dilemma of keeping his wife from finding the hooker who'd stayed in his apartment overnight.

Cosby welcomed the opportunity to do some slapstick in the silent-movie tradition. His co-star in the vignette was Richard Pryor, and it looked like it was to be an explosively funny combination of the smooth old pro and the skittery skinny young newcomer. They were to play doctors who, while on vacation with their wives, are hapless victims of a broken-down car, bad plumbing, and other hotel nightmares. But the trouble was that the director broke a key rule of slapstick comedy: The violence was humorless.

The climax of the segment begins on the tennis court, where the doctors and their wives get hit with balls and smack each other with tennis rackets. Unlike the old slapstick, where a Buster Keaton jumps back up after a fall, or a Curly Howard smack in the skull is accompanied by a weird sound effect, where violence perpetrated against Lou Costello is met with funny faces and screams, these bits were played straight. When one of the ladies trips over some balls and falls flat on her face, it's not funny. It looks like she could be hurt.

Back at the hotel room, hobbled by injuries, Pryor's wife smacks her head on the bathroom mirror—painfully. She knocks over a ninety-dollar bottle of perfume.

"Of all the stupid-ass things to do," grumbles Cosby.

"Hold on," Pryor shouts. "She did not do it on purpose."

"You mean it was a planned accident?"

The men start bickering, and it escalates rapidly. Pryor becomes a wild man, a rangy, half-insane little nut. Cosby remains the straight man, wary, awesome, and scowling. Pryor, in hysterics, threatens to bash Bill in the head with a tennis racket at the count of five. Cosby, in perfect control, barks, "Never threaten a man who spent two years working the drunk ward. Back off!" And when Pryor shivers, unable to find the courage to count the final five, Cosby goads him into it.

Pryor's puny attack is met by powerful Cosby arms. He hurls Pryor down, the tennis racket smacking into the TV set, blowing it out. Pryor charges again, only to be bounced off the far wall.

The madman rushes forward yet again and catches Cos around the legs. "Don't bite me," Cos warns sternly. "You could give me a blood disease!" In his frustration, he gathers little Richard up like a pile of laundry, and, exasperated beyond control, grabs the man's head, pulls it forward, and bites him on the nose.

When next observed, the two couples, all in bandages and casts, are trudging haplessly through the hotel lobby, the perfect vacation over.

The entire vignette was predictable, but could've been pretty funny. Cosby as a comic straight man and Pryor as his inane sidekick could've worked. It just wasn't executed properly, and most movie critics shrugged it off as such.

The critic from *The New Yorker,* Pauline Kael had a different point of view. The influential critic insisted that the movie was antiblack!

She pointed out that, onstage, white actors had played the Cosby-Pryor roles. She decided that "when the roles are played by black actors, the skit seems to be saying that the men may be doctors but they're still uncontrollable, dumb blacks."

Attacking the film's art direction (the hotel had white wallpaper and pastel-colored furnishings), she insisted that the men's blackness was deliberately distorted: "The recessive whitened decor turns them into tar babies."

As for the slapstick, the ineptness of the accident-prone duo proved that blacks "don't know how to handle cars. . . . When they stumble around a flooded room, crash into each other, step on broken glass, or, even worse, when Cosby bites Pryor's nose, it all has horrifying racist overtones."

Delivering a final blast in this very prominent, very important weekly magazine, Kael insisted the movie could "give offense to just about everyone," especially with its "glamorously unhappy Wasps . . . baggy-pants Jews, and blacks who act like clowning savages."

Talk about giving offense. When Dr. William H. Cosby, Jr., read the piece, his blood pressure could've been charted on the Richter scale. Taking out a full-page ad in *Variety,* he let his frustration drip from every line he wrote: "Are we to be denied a right to romp through hotels, bite noses, and, in general, beat up one another in the way Abbott & Costello, Laurel & Hardy, Martin & Lewis, Buster Keaton, and Charlie Chaplin did—and more recently as those actors in the movie *Animal House?* I heard no cries of racism in those reviews. If my work is not funny—it's not funny. But this industry does not need projected racism from critics."

The controversy stewed for days. The film's producer, Ray Stark, accused Kael of irresponsibility. Others simply dismissed the review as typical of a lady whose views seemed to veer drastically between scintillating and senile. Of the protests, Liz Smith said, "Kael probably won't care. She is used to being attacked."

Cosby was used to being attacked, too. But, to quote Bob Dylan's song about Lenny Bruce, Cos fought his war "on a battlefield where every victory hurt." Every step of the way, Cosby's triumphs as a comedian, as an actor, as a trailblazer for civil rights, as one of black America's most positive images—every step of the way Cosby heard criticism ranging from outrageous blasts to inane sniping, and much of it confusedly racist.

But whenever one avenue was blocked off, Cosby found another. His versatility enabled him to strike new fire in stand-up, on TV, in movies, on records—even as a singer. The moment he was stuck, he simply unstuck himself and changed direction—but he always moved forward.

Now he shifted gears in his movie career, returning to children's entertainment. He turned up next in Disney's *The Devil and Max Devlin.*

"That Walt Disney was the slickest guy who ever operated in this town," Cos once said. "Do you realize that for every three people who see a Disney picture, there are probably two who didn't really want to come to the theater? That's right. Parents go because that's something their kid can see. And, man, when you got one or two out of every three people going to the theater when they don't even want to be there, you got something going for you."

What a natural idea: Bill Cosby matched with Walt Disney. It was an idea whose time had come—too late. By the time Cosby arrived, the Disney Studios were losing prestige—and sometimes money—with their rigidly G-rated, mild live-action films.

If Cosby thought he could turn things around, so did his fans. Ads for *The Devil and Max Devlin* promised only slightly less excitement than *The Devil in Miss Jones.* With wickedly smiling Cosby and lovable clod Elliott Gould, the one-minute TV teasers promised a feast of devilish pranks. Sitting through the whole film turned out to be purgatory.

Gould plays a creepy landlord who evicts people on any pretext. Tripped by a blind old lady and sent sprawling into the gutter, he's run over by a truck full of Hare Krishnas. A colorful beginning, but the beginning of the end.

"Welcome to hell," an unsmiling Cosby intones. He's not the devil after all, but "Barney Satan," evidently one of the devil's soul brothers. Gould is justly awed by the sight of exploding fireballs and gaunt, corpse-white zombies. Cos lays out the plot: Gould will be restored to life if he can bring in three "fresh, unsullied, innocent" souls. The souls of three kiddies.

The plot is paced like a taffy pull. Gould tediously goes about his work, introducing himself to his adorable targets: Julie Budd, a kind of junior Barbra Streisand with searing lung power and an ambition to sell her soul for the chance to sing bad Marvin Hamlisch tunes; Sonny Shroyer, who would like to become a motorcyclist (and ride into somebody else's movie); and too-cute, pudding-bowl-coiffured Adam Rich, who might make a deal with the devil if it means getting a new papa for his knock-out mom, dour Susan Anspach.

Gould doesn't know if he can con all three kids. "Oh, God," he mutters. Cosby says, "I wish you wouldn't say that." And that's as witty as the script ever gets.

Though Gould and Cosby shared the billing, Gould had about seventy percent of the screen time. Cos was left to pop up now and then to see how Gould was doing, and he had no time to say anything more than "What about those contracts? . . . Your time is almost up."

Cosby was misused. Brief flashes show what *could've* been done. In one scene Cos teases Gould by popping up unexpectedly, pursing his lips in the famous Cosby smirk, and giving him the eye. Cosby could easily have played a lovable devil throughout. In another, even briefer moment, with Cosby losing patience, he delivers his lines with Sheldon Leonard menace and a baleful stare. This too could have been chillingly effective if it had been carried on throughout the film.

Instead the movie went from fun to funeral within the first five minutes, and Cosby was wasted—until the end. Then the film took a shocking turn for Cosby-watchers. It was obvious from the beginning that Gould would double-cross the devil. When he does, Cosby's hellish temper comes out. No longer is he wearing a business suit. Suddenly he blazes onto the screen as a hairy, red-legged satyr with woolly crimson goathair on his head and a bare chest. He shouts at Gould, "Burn those contracts and eternal damnation is yours! You'll know the unmitigating pain and horror of limbs torn from their sockets. You'll feel pain you never imagined in life, yours forever! Flesh you'll smell burn! Rotting forever!" It was a tantalizing peek at the rage Cosby is capable of showing, and it slips by in less than a minute.

Now that he had followed *California Suite* with another turkey, it looked like the only way Bill could get satisfaction in a film was if he wrote it, directed it, and starred in it himself. As for trying television again, Cos reflected, "I just haven't been able to put together the kind of show where the public will say, 'Hey, let's watch!' It's as simple as that." And in stand-up comedy, the leading attraction was still fiery Richard Pryor. Tastes were definitely turned toward the hothead and away from Cool Cos.

He was now forty-four, and it looked like the best of Bill Cosby's career, like the best of an aging sports star's career, was well behind him.

Chapter
18

"We comedians have a staying power of maybe twenty years," Cosby said, nearing his twentieth year in show business. "Unless we come up with something new, we can run out of welcome."

It seemed that the welcome mat was down for Cosby only on *The Tonight Show* and out on the road. Like others who had had TV series and lost them, or had movie careers and seen them peter out, Bill became one of those people called "celebrities," who, to the average TV viewer, don't seem to do much except sit around being a star. Bill joined comics like Don Rickles, Tony Randall, Buddy Hackett, and Shecky Greene in the ritual Carson interviews promoting club dates.

Now middle-aged, Cosby appeared to be coasting. He described slowing down in an article for *Ebony*. He wrote that he was having trouble keeping weight off, wasn't able to keep his body as finely tuned as he used to. As for such basics as food and sex, Bill felt these areas were also not going to get any better.

"When you reach middle age, you find that everything you eat turns to gas . . . your stomach changes, too, as to what it can and *will* accept." And in the bedroom, "you come home late . . . you get into bed and touch and start to make your move. She says, 'No,' and you roll back over the other way and say to yourself, 'Thank you so much,' because you were not all that serious in the first place. All you wanted to do was go on record. The first thing you say at breakfast the next morning is, 'You know, I made my move last night, and *you* weren't ready.' "

Cos complained that, aside from the body, the memory was going too. He'd walk into a room and forget what he'd come in for. And he'd get mad at himself for forgetting. "There are, of course, some advantages that occur in middle age," he wrote. "But now that I'm forty and my mind has started to play tricks on me, I can't remember what they are."

On *The Tonight Show,* audiences saw him wearing glasses more often. One time he admitted that he would probably have a long life, even if it included needing thicker glasses. He mentioned that his grandfather lived to be ninety-eight years old.

"But they were taking pieces away from him," Cosby added. "They cut his legs off. He had diabetes. And my Aunt Clara went in and she said, 'Oh, Daddy, you've lost your legs!' And he said, 'Be quiet. You didn't say anything when they took all my teeth.' And that was important to him. Your teeth go, then your legs, and they were just chipping away at him, so he said, 'I think I better leave.' "

Carson asked, "Does aging bother you?"

"No," Cos answered evenly, "it doesn't bother me at all. I'm just happy to be here no matter what the punishment."

The punishment appeared to be parenthood, the main theme of many of his monologues. More than ever, Cos was reaching out to all those fans from the sixties who were now parents themselves—and coming back to Cos to hear all about what they'd let themselves in for. That included kids whose favorite words were *I dunno* and *mine* and having to talk like a tobacco auctioneer to get them to "Stop it stop it stopit-stopitstopit."

"Some people are disappointed because I still do a family show," Cos said, "but if something pulls and holds a family together, and makes them laugh at themselves . . . that's a part of life I want to give."

Cosby's interest in children's programming was still high, and, though some fans were hardly aware of it, Cos was involved with Bob "Captain Kangaroo" Keeshan and the *Weekly Reader* in producing *Picture Pages,* a series of five-minute video shows helping preschoolers to learn to read.

Most were aware of Cos for all those commercials he did with kids. Sure, kids loved Cos, but he clued folks in on those Jell-O ads: "The kids really respond to me . . . well, you know how they do that? They get about five hundred kids in a room before I even get into the building, and they show them me in *Electric Company* tapes, and they watch the five hundred for the five kids who are most turned on . . . and they grab them and give them to me for the ad. The rest is easy."

Cosby had become another Mr. Whipple or Josephine the Plumber, a famous funny character in commercials. But even here, Cos had to worry a little. After being named *Advertising Age*'s "Star Presenter of 1978," Cos was dropped by one of his major clients, Ford Motors, in 1979. While he was doing Ford commercials, their sales had gone up from 2.3 million to 2.6 million, but a new ad agency had come in and someone had said, "We'll let the products be the stars." There was a hint that Cos had overextended himself.

In the summer of 1981, Cos made an appearance at the Kool Jazz Festival, where he was invited to put together an informal "dream concert" of some of his favorites. Bill assembled Arnett Cobb on sax, Jimmy Smith on keyboards, Mickey Roker on drums, and B. B. King for guitar and vocals.

"This is a happening," he said happily. "It's for people who love jazz and love to laugh and love to have a good time." He saw a definite link between comedy, his way, and playing jazz. "With B. B. King you know the song, you want him to sing it, but each time he is constantly challenged to hit it right," and yet make it come out fresh and different. Cos would write out material on a yellow legal pad, but always improvised from there, never doing the same bits the same way.

Guest-hosting *The Tonight Show*, Cos continued to give airtime to favorite jazz performers like Dizzy Gillespie and Sonny Rollins, but was disappointed that there wasn't much new comedy talent, anyone with "a good five minutes." He'd visit East and West Coast comedy shops, but the clientele were mostly vacant-eyed yuppies and the only way comics could reach them was through inane shock comedy.

The new rage in stand-up was young Eddie Murphy, who turned out to be a cross between the outrageous Richard Pryor and cool, likable Cos. Murphy did both of them, starting out doing "a salute to Richard Pryor" with bits copped from records, and eventually perfecting a Cosby impression complete with vested suit, wire-rimmed glasses, cigar, and self-satisfied smile.

Murphy recalls his first contact with the real thing: "Bill Cosby called me up and said, 'You can't get onstage and say fuck you.' That was the most bizarre thing that's happened in my career. Bill Cosby calling me up and reprimanding me for being too dirty. Wow."

But Eddie has great respect for Bill. He follows a little of the Cosby lifestyle: He doesn't smoke cigarettes, drink, or use drugs. "You never hear any garbage about Cosby," says Murphy. "He has a happy home life."

Meanwhile Murphy and Pryor continued to dominate in comedy. Cosby's audience wasn't really theirs. Bill knew "the young swingers would probably be the most difficult for me as an audience, because my act is not designed to cover lovemaking or sex; it's designed for the philosophy of people who are thinking of having a family, or already have one."

Cos wasn't about to hip-up his style to accommodate the hard-core element in the audience. "Let's say that what Bill Cosby does, he is known for. And the people who like him, like him for that."

In the family arenas where he began to play, the concert halls and suburban theaters, Cosby became a family institution in stand-up, another George Burns or Jack Benny. He could take ten or twenty minutes for a leisurely warm-up, and the audience would wait with respect and devotion. Cos developed a friendship with the crowd that went against the traditional "kill the audience" hysteria of many frantic and hostile comics:

"I used to want to destroy people with laughter. I wanted to make their stomachs hurt. But that isn't fair. It really hurts and it makes people tired. So now I pace myself. I don't want people concentrating on their pain rather than their laughter."

A review at the time, from the *Daily Iowan,* described his heartland strength: "There were times when the jokes became obvious, when everyone knew what was coming. But the way he said things, the tone of voice, made predictable lines belly-splitters. . . . His delivery was timed with deadly accuracy." Simple lines were "delivered so marvelously" that the audiences were roaring with laughter. On paper it has almost no impact, but when Cosby, after a long lecture from his dad on how hard money is to come by, gets to the punchline, the audience howls. All he says is: "I did not ask you, 'Have you suffered, old man?' I asked you . . . for some money!"

"Bill Cosby is nothing less than the most gifted monologist of our time," Steve Allen has written. "One of the reasons . . . is that he is, richly and purposely and openly, the most childish," reaching "the child that each of us was, the child that still lives within us."

He does it with a limitless array of voices, faces, cadences, movements, not to mention his own inimitable delivery, where the words come out like they're being coaxed, shoved forward with a little bit of wobbly wonder and good-natured surprise.

Yet for all the adulation, Cosby has never rested on audience acceptance. He's aware of the nature of each different crowd: "You have to work differently in different places, but you still have to be Bill Cosby. Take Lake Tahoe. That's a family crowd . . . I can do a loose show and they'll stay with me. Vegas is something else . . . the people are intimidated. They've paid to have a good time . . . the prices are so high . . . I do a tighter show. I don't digress as much. It's like driving a car. Sometimes you make all the lights, sometimes you go bumper-to-bumper, but you still get there."

But in the eighties, Vegas wasn't the attraction it once was. By attrition, there were less fans for old-fashioned acts like Wayne Newton or Engelbert Humperdinck; more people were going to rock concerts or simply staying home. The co-owner of the Aladdin Hotel, John Jenkins, sulked, "Which of these lousy monkeys is worth $300,000 a week?"

Cosby, playing the Vegas Hilton at the time, was furious. But he answered "the terrible slur" with his brand of honesty, dignity, and self-respect. "I'm proud of my drawing record. It's up there with the best of them. I would never ask for more than I'm worth, but it's not fair to get less." With cool logic, he pointed out that it was Vegas club owners who ballooned star salaries in bidding wars, and it was their problem in failing to understand the public's point of view on entertainment value.

Often Cosby declined concert dates in favor of appearing at schools. As he told a writer from *Essence,* "In many of the lower economic areas, people constantly say that the children have no positive images. So they ask entertainers to come out and give speeches." He found that the kids were not interested in hearing Cosby lecture on staying in school or staying off drugs. They wanted to know how many cars he had and how big his house was. Bill would tell the kids that they had their own positive images to look for: "Look at your mother . . . see how she has to get up and do your clothing, do your food, give you money so that you can have something for lunch. Then she goes out and works and comes home to fix your dinner. What kind of image is that?" He felt it was important for kids to understand their parents a little more, be more aware of what it takes to raise a child.

At the Cosby home, he maintained a firm, loving hand. Sometimes the technique was a threat, sometimes just a logical discussion. As his monologues describe, sometimes nothing worked. But often, all that was needed was a little more communication and attention between parent and child.

Being on the road was tough. When Cos took his kids with him, the results were almost predictable: "Ennis—I don't know what got into him—but he was bored and he went out on the roof of the hotel, and he just wanted to see what would happen to Coca-Cola bottles . . . that were full . . . and the security guards came up and Coca-Cola was all over the place and they said, 'There's a little boy up there throwing bombs at the people.' And I didn't know it was my child. After that I had to keep him with me, and talk to him.''

All the Cosby kids turned out well. Erika Cosby, at age eighteen, turned out exceptionally well. She posed for fashion photos in the June 1983 issue of *Harper's Bazaar.* "Even though there was so little time," she reflected, "we feel very close to our dad. There's a special bond among us. You know, fathers just have a way of putting everything together."

Late in the year, Cosby teamed up with Sammy Davis, Jr., to create a blockbuster show that he figured even the slightly diminished Vegas crowd couldn't ignore. And he was right. The team of Sammy and Cos was hot stuff in the hot town.

They decided to continue the triumph and take the show to Broadway—the only facet of show business Cosby had not tried before. Sammy insisted that Broadway would be a fantastic experience.

Talking about *Sammy and Cos,* Broadway's two-man show, Cosby told Johnny Carson, "We went to Broadway and *bombed.* We had about seventeen people sitting there, man."

"How do you explain that?" Carson asked.

"Well, it was Sammy's fault," Cos deadpanned. "He wasn't drawin' at all. My people were there."

"Maybe," Carson began apologetically, "they just weren't used to seeing two performers on a legitimate stage."

"Maybe," Cos answered, "they just weren't interested!"

Actually fans were interested, but they wanted to pay five bucks, not fifty. And they were getting what they wanted, thanks to a new phenomenon called the "live in-concert" movie. Richard Pryor had been incredibly successful filming his stage act so everybody could see it, and cheaply. In the same way that rock videos brought the music industry out of the doldrums, these performance movies made stand-up comics suddenly in demand.

At one time stand-up acts were barely tolerated for seven minutes on *The Ed Sullivan Show;* now audiences wanted seventy minutes of a comedian's shtick. Cable TV offered Eddie Murphy, Buddy Hackett, George Burns, and Robin Williams in concert. Every year, the ratings got higher, videocassette versions were demanded, and the stars made more money. Robin Williams, for example, received $25,000 for his first special in 1978. In 1983, his price went to $750,000.

If Richard Pryor could do it, and Eddie Murphy, why not try the original . . . Bill Cosby himself?

With the national release of his performance film, *Bill Cosby Himself,* Cos emerged from what the public considered "semi-retirement." In a loose show that Cos also directed, the comedian covered some familiar territory, offering his brilliant "Dentist" routine, and some other material from his *My Father Confused Me* album—from a hysterical dissection of parental threats to his father's whimsical way of letting out gas: "Come here and pull my finger."

Cos was up to date with some satire on cocaine: "I asked a guy, 'What is it about cocaine that makes it so wonderful?'

" 'Well, it intensifies your personality.'

"I said, 'Yes, but what if you're an asshole?' "

Cosby's brilliance at pantomime was evident in his routine about drunks walking, and happy babies wriggling, and the bizarre squinting and staring doctors do while they view a woman in the stirrups about to give birth. His genius with sound was highlighted in "The Dentist": He imitated a dribbly patient with Novocained lips, the sound of drills, and the various gurgles and gasps of an open-mouthed victim of modern dentistry.

Most of the show was about becoming a parent (it started when Cosby saw his first child: "They washed it off and it wasn't getting any better. . . . I said to the doctor, 'Can you put this back? It's not done yet' ") and then enduring parenthood (including a nighttime three-child brawl over flipping towels and sudsing faces in the shower). "Parents are not interested in justice," he concluded. "They want quiet." Quiet from kids' screaming and crying and acting "brain-damaged" and answering every question with "I don't know."

The movie was generally greeted with enthusiasm. "I know it's hard to keep pushing yourself into different areas," Cos admitted, "but you have to if you want to be around in a few years. In this business, if you stand still, you disappear."

Cos, who seemed on the verge of disappearance, who hadn't had a TV show of his own in eight years, was now about to try television again. He was about to make one of the most explosive comebacks in TV history. And this time, he surprised everybody—even himself.

Chapter

19

Cosby was home watching TV. He didn't watch much of it. He tried to get his kids to refrain too, and to read more instead. "I decided to stay up and watch what was on cable. That night I saw three movies about rape. They all seemed designed to do the same thing—show women having their clothes torn off. . . . The next night I watched again. This time I heard people cursing for no reason other than to get a laugh. . . . Next I began to monitor the networks and the independent stations: women degraded, cops-and-robbers shows with the guns getting bigger and bigger."

He took it all in and said, "I'm tired of shows that consist of a car crash, a gunman, and a hooker talking to a black pimp." But had the public tired of it, too?

Over the past dozen years, Cosby had only appeared on TV in two shows; both were "family-oriented" and both were disasters. He told writer Bill Davidson that he approached the networks offering "a detective show . . . I would solve crimes with my wits, as Columbo once did, and my girlfriend would be a strong woman with her own career." There would be "no guns, no violence, no car chases." The networks said, "No way."

Cos thought it over again, going back to the basics of his entertainment career. He would do something truthful, something from the heart.

His new sitcom would be the real Cosby, out there and vulnerable, doing humor about human beings—a family's love and understanding. He'd do the kind of bits NBC executive Brandon Tartikoff saw him do on *The Tonight Show,* talking about his problems as a parent. It would be scheduled together with Tartikoff's pet project *Family Ties.* Basically the tone of the show would not be that different from Cosby's first situation comedy, with its emphasis on low-key slice-of-life vignettes.

As teacher Chet Kincaid, he handled students' problems and his own imperfections and foibles. As obstetrician-gynecologist Heathcliff Huxtable, he would handle his five kids' problems, and share the chores with his wife, a practicing lawyer. But he'd be laid-back, "a man in search of a perfect nap." And he'd have his hands full, being "not as in control as I pretend."

ABC and NBC were both interested. Cosby still had a tremendous "likability quotient," thanks to his commercials—and for commercial TV, that was a big, big selling point. But the networks were still worried about a show based on "warm, gentle humor." Was Don Quixote Cosby again galloping toward his "quality family show" vision—only to discover that the viewers for it were just a mirage? Cos played it charming and cool. On starting up the show, he said, "We have about six television sets in our house, and it's less expensive for me to do a television series than it is for me to throw them all out." He wanted to do the show in New York. "If I'm canceled," he said, "I'd like to be a little closer to home."

ABC backed off. NBC held on, but only wanted six episodes. That way they could cut their losses and bury Cos if the show was the same failure his 1976 one was. They weren't even sure of Cosby's name: Heathcliff Huxtable. *Heathcliff* was okay, kind of funny. But *Huxtable* was uppity. They asked him to change the name to Brown.

Cosby discovered that some things never changed. His "game face" came on. He took a hard line. He wanted total control and would accept nothing less. He wanted at least thirteen weeks to get his show going, not six. Meanwhile, NBC scrutinized old tapes of his *Tonight Show* appearances. They were looking for Cosby the family man. They found some of it in his new stand-up routines:

"One of the things you learn when you become a parent is the horrible thought and the reality that your children will *be* your children for the rest of your life! That's why there's death."

Cosby described an incident at home with his eight-year-old daughter Evin: "I just finished eating and my stomach was swollen from the food that went in it. And she patted me on the stomach and said, 'Dad, you have a big stomach.' I tried to give her wisdom and so I said, 'Dad's stomach is full of food, that's why it looks this way.'

"She said, 'Yes, and you have a big nose because you don't pick it.' "

Cos had a glazed smile on his face as he added, "I don't like her anymore . . . but she's too cute to throw out."

NBC was amused, but, just to make sure, they insisted Cosby do a short pilot show. Knowing the network mind, Cos decided to film a vignette of Dr. Huxtable talking to his daughters about sex. This got NBC's attention and slowly the concessions came. NBC even found a studio in Brooklyn for Cos.

Before long, the studio set was redone in Cosby's image. By now Cos had a permanent Big Apple residence as well as the Amherst and California homes, and was about to buy a house outside Philadelphia, too. Dr. Huxtable's home would be a replica of Cosby's townhouse. Duplicates of Cosby's Oriental rugs, antiques, Queen Anne chairs, and the rest were made, and the walls held paintings by a favorite artist of Bill's, Varnette Honeywood.

The Brooklyn studio itself had a down-to-earth feel to it. Located about an hour away from midtown Manhattan (up to two hours if anybody's going by subway) the square brick building was smack in the middle of a quiet, suburban part of the borough. There were a few prewar apartment buildings nearby, but most of the streets were flat with rows of humble two-story houses, some peeled and worn and in the throes of neglect, others sporting fresh paint, new gates and fences, and other signs of urban renewal. Down the street from the studio on Avenue M and Fourteenth were a humble fruit stand, a hot bagel place, and a cluttered newsstand—nothing fancier for the *Cosby Show* staff, nor for the cast of *Another World,* who also used the obscure Brooklyn facility.

Behind the scenes, Cosby got involved in endless story conferences, total rewrites, a dissection of each script for motivation and realism. Cosby's eldest daughter Erika was away at Princeton; the character corresponding to her, Sondra, would be away at college too for the first episodes. Each script was treated to an almost psychiatric appraisal. There was even a real psychiatrist on hand as an adviser, Harvard University's Dr. Alvin Poussaint.

The show had to be faithful to Cosby's attitudes toward life and comedy. He cautioned his racially mixed writing staff to stay away from sitcom cliché. "If this was 1964," he said, "my wife could do the cooking and I could be the guy on the sofa who just says, 'Let your mother handle this.' But today a lot of things have changed and I want the show to reflect those changes. A family where the father cooks, too, and pitches in with the kids, and where everyone has responsibilities."

Guiding the show along, Cosby once again seemed to shoulder most of the burdens. "I feel a great responsibility," he admitted, "to make it as good and as real as I can." Cosby's standards were so tough that three writers quit after the first six episodes. The hectic rewriting and clashing over focus and nuance caused head writer Earl Pomerantz to quit, too. "Bill challenges you to do your best," he said, "but I must say that I was awfully tired." Cosby's humor always came from richly defined characters and situations, not from one-liners and cheap sight gags. It was hard to turn out half hours with as much polish and charm as Cosby's ten-minute monologues.

"I said to the writers I don't want sitcom jokes. I don't want jokes about behinds or breasts or pimples or characters saying 'Oh my God' every other line. What we want to deal with is human behavior." Save the wisecracks for *Webster* and *Diff'rent Strokes, Benson* and *Gimme a Break.* Save the leering for John Ritter and the plastic gags for the plastic yuppies on shows like *Night Court.*

Meanwhile reports on Cosby's family show about upper-middle-class blacks met with the laughter of derision. While he worked on deadline, keeping a close watch on the show's characters, comedy, and quality, he had to deal with the doubting, pessimistic reporters.

Bill, why do a family show? Aren't you out of touch? How many whites will be on the show? Will you show the *real* black American family? What about social problems? What about white *versus* black? Isn't it a fairy tale to portray blacks as doctors and lawyers? How come you don't talk like George Jefferson or Fred Sanford—isn't that real black dialect? And why aren't you having the family live in the ghetto?

"All we're trying to show all America is that in a lot of ways behavior is the same all over," Cos would say, again and again. It was like twenty years ago when he said, "Let's talk about the similarities, not the differences." But people weren't listening.

All they did was complain. And each reporter had a definite point of view about how blacks were in real life, and how they should be portrayed on TV, and Cosby was supposed to agree with every single one.

"Why do they want to deny me the pleasure of being an American and just enjoying life?" Bill asked. "Why must I make all the black social statements?" Why not do a show *his* way, "a class way . . . something to be proud of . . . to show that we have the same kinds of wants and needs as other American families."

Looking at sitcoms in the 1980s, the cycle between so-called "blacks in whiteface" and "funky soul families" had spun way off course. New shows had smart blacks—who played maids and butlers to doltish whites. A bizarre fad had almost abnormal black children acting extraterrestrially superior to the white families that adopted them. The only holdover from the previous decade was *The Jeffersons,* with its gleeful reverse racism and "honky this" and "honky that." And now Cosby was already getting heat for simply showing his conception of a normal, upper-middle-class black family. Not a fake family based on fairy tale—*his* family.

And nobody believed him. People doubted him. Twenty years later he was still answering race questions. Twenty years and he was still fighting negativity, still defending his style of comedy. Two decades and too many questions. Cosby'd had enough.

At a press conference he told reporters that he would answer only to himself. As for the upper-middle-class black family bit: "My wife plays a lawyer," he enunciated, "and I'm a doctor. For those of you who have a problem with that . . . that's *your problem.*"

Uh-oh. Boy, Bill's a little touchy, isn't he?

No, not touchy. Bill Cosby is *arrogant!*

The Cosby Show had barely been on the air for a month when a damaging cover story on Bill appeared in *TV Guide.* Its title was a warning: WITNESS THE HUMORS OF BILL COSBY. Writer Kathleen Fury said her interview with Cos "was unpleasant. He made no attempt to be amiable and was by turns combative, defensive, challenging, threatening and hostile . . . one of the most arrogant celebrities I've ever met."

Was this just a case of the wrong writer interviewing the wrong star at the wrong time? Was it a misreading of a star's protective ego or a comedian's innate anger? Was it the pressure of Cosby's responsibility for his show?

If it was, Ms. Fury reasoned, then Cosby wasn't as intelligent as his Ph.D. claimed—he should've been smart enough to answer her questions politely. He'd refused to talk about his father when she asked him why she hadn't heard much about him lately. (One reason was that he was now deceased.) Cosby intimidated her by grousing about an old *TV Guide* article that dared mention how many cars he owned. She called him "clamlike" for his concern about privacy. Though the writer seemed to get enough mainstream quotes for her piece, the experience was a trial. She did seem to think Cosby's ego had to come from the almost worshipful reverence people held for him. When she was on the street with him, he was mobbed by cheering, devoted fans. But he was rude then, too. After signing autographs over and over, "for some reason known only to him, he stopped."

Looking for other signs of Cosby arrogance, she gave him a kick below the belt: "While educated people talked Zero Population Growth, he and his wife had five children."

The piece caused an immediate stir, and was quoted by many disgruntled newspapers that had failed to secure private interviews with the increasingly wary Cosby. *Us* magazine couldn't get to Bill, so they quoted *TV Guide*. *Newsweek* admitted they too were turned down, so they also quoted *TV Guide*'s arrogance line. But thirty million people seem to think that, whatever his moods at times, Cosby is still a very funny fellow. Even as *TV Guide* hit the stands, Cosby's show hit number one, one of the biggest upsets in TV history.

Who could have predicted it? Not Cos.

On *The Tonight Show* with guest host Joan Rivers, Cos said he was surprised by his success. He'd only hoped to post enough numbers to keep the show going. After all, the deck had been so stacked against him. Not only were sitcoms on the decline and smutty soap operas favored over family fare, Cos's competition was *Magnum, P.I.,* a powerhouse detective show with great appeal: Kids and fans of violence loved it; women loved Tom Selleck, and some men loved him too. But now *Magnum* was dumped and Cos was king. In one eleven-week stretch, he was number one nine times. Once in a while *Dynasty* or *Dallas* would nudge him out, but even blockbusters had a tough time. The Super Bowl beat him, but he beat the Academy Awards.

"Yeah, it feels good," he told Rivers. "It's like seeing a fat pitch comin' down the middle and you have a big bat!" Johnny Carson joked about his success. "It's number one in the ratings," he said one night during his monologue. "Now I hear they're trying to get Prince and Tina Turner for a remake of *Ozzie and Harriet*."

The critics began to side with Cosby. *People* called the show "revolutionary" and now called *The Jeffersons* "an obnoxious parody of white upward mobility." *Newsday* also compared the two, saying, "The Jeffersons are rich. But they are absurdly nouveau riche. The Dr. Cosby family . . . are upper middle. And they belong there. This is a real breakthrough." *The New York Times* enthused: "Mr. Cosby, here at his very best, can take the ordinary and make it seem delightfully fresh."

But there was the *Village Voice*. Referring to Dr. Huxtable, black gynecologist, they wrote, "If anything is going to awaken the well-buried racism of genteel America, it's the notion of black fingers messing with their womanhood's collective Down There."

A mark of success for a TV show is when it gets parodied in *Mad* magazine. But this time, some of the satire was sour. In true *Mad* tradition, *The Cosby Show* became *The Clodsby Show*, and Cliff Huxtable "Quippin Yockstable." Cos took a ribbing for his endless *Tonight Show* appearances (he was shown with a medical text on "Terminal Carsonoma") and his commercials (his most pressing emergency call was not from a patient, but somebody from Coca-Cola). The show was lampooned for its cuteness. There was a caricature of Cosby with little Keshia Knight Pulliam. "Isn't that the most adorable living doll . . . look at those incredibly cute facial expressions." It turned out the speakers were talking about Cosby.

But the ugly ethnic jokes were totally out of place. The son is punched and develops "a white eye." He's made to say, "If we're black how come we're so well off? How come we act white . . . and *think* white?"

Cosby was still getting flak for his mainstream point of view. And now that he wasn't even defending himself by trying to talk to the press, he was continuing to get blasted. Even if he *was* succeeding on TV as a nice guy, he was still pretty arrogant in person.

In *Jet*, Cosby was quoted on the problem: "That makes me sound like a real bad guy, doesn't it? But I turned down requests because the magazines said they wouldn't put me on their covers. Is that arrogant? I see so many magazine covers featuring blood and violence and sex. I didn't think it was an unreasonable request, since our show deals with important family relationships."

When he appeared live on *The Phil Donahue Show*, viewers could see how deeply disturbed Bill was by the negative remarks and his constant need to defend his positions. He had been joking with the audience, taking time to explain his point of view on his production of a family show filled with gentle humor, when members of the audience began to ask about blacks versus whites.

What about breaking the cycle of "all-white television"? What about "black girls running and hugging on white guys" and rock videos where black men are with white girls? Cosby's face clouded with anger. "I would like to right now stop with this program," he said. "I am not an authority on blackness. I didn't come on this program to discuss blackness. I came on this show to discuss human beings and let's get into that. . . . I don't want to spend the time when a black person shows up on a show talking about blackness and what you all have to do in order to make America better. When Bob Newhart comes on here let's have him talk about it. When whatever person comes on let's have them talk about it. Right now, why don't you see if I can be a h-u-m-a-n b-e-i-n-g." The audience applauded.

Meanwhile applause for *The Cosby Show* grew. And with all the laughter on the show, and the confusing negative remarks in the press about Cosby, some viewers had to wonder: "Is the Bill Cosby I see on *The Cosby Show* the *real* Bill Cosby?"

"The character he's playing," Robert Culp told *Newsweek,* "is very close to the real Bill Cosby. He's taken off all the veils."

Roy Silver, as his ex-manager, in a perfect position to sound off, instead insists, "Bill Cosby was and is intrinsically funny. If you sat in a car with him and drove from New York to Philadelphia, he'd have you in hysterics. In many ways he's really remarkable. He never drinks. He never did drugs. Married to the same wife, has five kids, well-spoken, articulate, sincere—my God—charismatic. What else could you want?"

Ernie Casale, Bill's athletic director at Temple, expressed surprise when told about the "arrogance" rap. Is the Cos we see on TV the real Cosby? "Oh, yes," he says, "that's Cosby. Once you get to know him, his actions are the same, you can tell. The things he says, the way he moves. People are seeing him—that's Cosby.

"I've never seen Bill as an arrogant person. I've seen him go out of his way to be nice to people all the time. I can't believe that. God, he'll do anything to please people when he's around us."

Bill visits Temple regularly, and Casale insists that, even in private situations, without the spotlight, Cosby is down to earth. Once, when he and Bill were at an airport in Houston, "a crowd gathered, and Bill and I sat there, and he just practically put on a show for these people. He didn't say, 'Let's get out of here' or anything like that. And I just thought it was so damn nice that he would do that. So I can't appreciate people saying he's arrogant. I've walked with him, I've seen him stop talking with me and go over and talk with some kids, up and down Broad Street. One day there was a kid in a wheelchair, and Bill went over and started pushing the wheelchair, asking him where he wanted to go. Now maybe you might say he did that because I was there, but I don't think so. That's Bill."

That's Bill, every week on TV. In showing life with the Huxtable family, he shows a great deal about his own reactions around the Cosby house—from cute to conservative, from confused to curmudgeonly to comical. The audience picked up on him so strongly that the show was actually getting bigger ratings when it went into reruns in the spring! NBC posted some big numbers, and most credited Cosby's number one for leading the charge back. "I want it known it was me who saved NBC!" Cos joked.

Describing his vindication as an advocate of family TV, Cosby called his success "a major, major step, not just for the American people but for those who control what goes on the air. The truth is in the numbers, and this helps straighten out nonbelievers concerning what an American audience will watch."

By the time the final episodes were ready to go, Cos was committed to doing another new sitcom about warmth, love and problem-solving, with the fiercely sincere Tony Orlando as star. Cos was ready to gamble further, that audiences were not only responding to Cosby, but the entire "family" concept. Orlando was written into an episode in order to introduce him to the public. The funniest thing about the show occurred in rehearsal. After Tony muffed a line during a romantic love scene, Cos ran up to him with a big piece of cardboard and started fanning him below the waist.

Aside from Orlando, Cos had many of his friends on the show in that first year—Clarence Williams III, Lena Horne, and even Dizzy Gillespie, as a music teacher. One of the most affecting episodes was the one that brought Sheldon Leonard back before the cameras. As the hospital's administrator, he was going to give Dr. Huxtable an award. Actually, his speech was more an award to Bill Cosby. He talked about hiring minorities only "because they had talent." Then he said, "About twenty years ago I recruited a young doc named Heathcliff Huxtable. He was a diamond in the rough . . . but to prove how good my judgment is in people, he has turned out to be extraordinary . . . he brings to his patients a degree of empathy and compassion that is very hard to match."

Then a joke to knock the edge off: "His dedication to this hospital is so great that, whenever business in the maternity ward slowed down, his wife came in pregnant."

On many TV shows, once a script is done, that's it; no changes. But according to *The Cosby Show*'s head writer and co-executive producer, John Markus, "We're always changing things, trying to make them better and better. The actors read them, then we make changes after that, and keep on adding and taking away." Lines are altered up to the final taping, and even beyond. If Cos feels, during performance, that another line might work better, he'll go with the feeling.

The Cosby Show goes through a triple polishing. First there are the rehearsals. These are long days, and, as Markus points out, even the Cosby kids are not immune: "They work really hard. They have to do three hours of school a day, about fifteen hours a week. And then they have to rehearse, so between rehearsing and going to school, their day is from ten to six in the evening." Then there's the double and triple polishing when the show is taped *twice* on Thursday evenings. Each half-hour show takes two weeks to write, a week to rehearse, and four hours to film. "We use four cameras," says Markus, "and they're going simultaneously. The director can select all the angles he wants, editing as the cameras are moving." The best takes from the two shows are edited together for one complete episode.

The Cosby Show is the hottest ticket in New York, and both tapings play to a packed studio audience. The audience files in about an hour before actual taping begins. They're "warmed up" with the help of a stand-up comic hired for the occasion, followed by a tape of another week's show, and a question-answer session done by one of the writers, the producer, or Cosby himself. One week it's John Markus answering the questions: "Who's Dr. William H. Cosby, Jr.?" "That's Bill!" "I have a photo, can I get Bill to autograph it?" "That's . . . tough . . . because of all the work we have to do. I'm afraid we don't have time." "How many shows do you do a year?" "We do twenty-five shows." "Where is the house they use when they film Cliff coming home?" "That was done on the East Side of Manhattan someplace. The Huxtables live in Brooklyn, but it could be any place in the boroughs. . . ."

During lulls in shooting, when technical problems arise, one of the staff will continue answering questions, but sometimes Bill himself drops by.

"In that scene where you were eating scrambled eggs," a member of the audience asks, "was that real food?"

"We always use real food," Cos answers. And that can be a problem. "When I was on *I Spy*, there was a scene that called for me to eat some Japanese food. Now I *love* Japanese food, so I ate a lot of it. Then we had to do the scene over. I was already stuffed, but I had to continue eating until we got the scene right. I didn't feel too good later."

"Do you really drink Coke?" someone shouts.

"Yes!" Cos mock-shouts back. Besides, Cos knows firsthand how they make the stuff: he and Julius "Dr. J" Erving are part owners of the company's bottling plant in Philly.

The audience sits in front of the three main sets. In the left corner, there's the bedroom. In the center there's the spacious kitchen and next door, the living room. Of course, when people climb upstairs to the second floor, they have to stop. There *is* no upstairs. The hallway and the children's rooms are stage right, almost out of sight of the studio audience.

The cameras slide across the floor from set to set. Each scene is usually fairly short, from two to five minutes, starting with a character entering the living room or kitchen, and finishing when a character leaves. Doing short sequences lets the actors refresh themselves by restudying the script, but after a week's rehearsal, they've got their lines down pat. That doesn't mean they can get them *out* without an occasional mumble or fumble. There could easily be a half-hour show of outtakes alone.

Six-year-old Keshia, the youngest cast member, has mischievous eyes and a winning smile, and when she delivers a cute line she sometimes can't help smiling as the audience laughs. When she gets an attack of the giggles, Cos is very much in character: He grabs hold of her and pretends to throttle her, telling the audience, "We're going to lose a kid after this shooting, so you all explain to your neighbors why the kid died."

In a scene between Bill and Malcolm Jamal Warner, an alarm clock is supposed to go off, waking the boy up. Bill hovers at his son's bedside, waiting for the alarm clock to buzz. He smiles. He waits. His smile gets sillier and sillier, stretching broadly across his face. Finally he breaks up and says, "Let's start again. The clock's broken on the first take!"

When the audience is in on a flub like that, the laughter gets louder when the action is done right. Viewers at home might think there are prompting lights on the set (no, not a single applause sign) or that artificial laughter has been added. But when Malcolm glides past Cosby in one scene, bumping into a chair and stumbling, and he has to do the scene over, there's natural appreciative laughter when he simply strolls by without knocking into anything.

Sometimes the laughter continues well after a scene is shot. After a breakfast sequence, Cosby and the crew are about to shift to the living room set. Suddenly Cos rushes back, swoops down, and swipes a bowl of cereal off the breakfast table. His eyes go large, then he grins impishly and starts eating big spoonfuls of cereal, guarding the bowl and trotting far away from the giggling cast members, and little Keshia, who tries to grab her bowl back.

With the short taping sequences interrupted by changes of costume, technical checks, and the replacement of cameras, the cast will often sit around in the living room quietly reading their scripts over, like a family sharing the Sunday paper. They go over particular points together, sometimes breaking up over some spontaneous gag. With time to kill, Cos sometimes wanders around the set, very much the informal host, sharing a word or two with a crew member or checking a technical point. Most of the time he's neither conspicuously "on," trying to force laughter, nor at the other extreme, grimly "off" and bored. He's as casual as any worker in an average office, talking to co-workers, taking an interest in all phases of the work but not letting himself get too wound up. While waiting for a scene to be set, he walks past the lights and pauses in the darkness near the first row of the studio audience. "It's nice and cool back here," he says. Then he moves back.

By the last scene, though, the irrepressible gremlin in Cos slips out again. This is a bedroom scene. The cameras and crew are there and the rest of the set is dark. When Cos comes in from the makeup room backstage, he stumbles through the living room in his long nightgown, calling out "I can't see back here!" And he begins to howl like a Halloween ghost, moving slowly through the eerie empty set, going "Whoooo, aah-wooo," in a deep, low, funereal voice. The audience goes into hysterics as the somnambulist spirit lumbers toward the bedroom. But once he gets there, abruptly the ghostly siren goes off and Cos is all business, taking his place and waiting for his cue.

Dr. Cosby knows when enough's enough. He disciplines himself and the rest of the cast. When the breakups get to be too much, he'll mock-glower and say, "Come on, we want to get home before Saturday," or shout an all-business "Let's get it together" to bring everyone back to professional reality.

"Working with Bill is like learning from a master," says Lisa Bonet. Sometimes when problems come up both professionally and personally, she goes to her TV parent for advice.

Some of the kids routinely call him Dad, while others call him just plain Bill. Bill's real-life children have met their TV counterparts informally, at visits to the Cosby home in Amherst. The kids seem to get along pretty well, though comparisons can be a problem. Take Cosby's son Ennis and his TV-show son Malcolm Jamal Warner: Ennis is about six-four, and Malcolm is five-six. When they played basketball together, it was no contest.

Well into the first season, Malcolm said, "It's still coming to me that I'm working with *the* Bill Cosby, the same Bill Cosby who has been around for twenty years. He has a nice personality. He's funny. He acts like a parent and a friend." The two went on a "father-and-son" trip to Atlantic City, where Malcolm saw Bill perform. They've a lot in common, especially the way they behaved in public school. Malcolm is tutored now, but if he were in a classroom situation, he admits he'd be like Bill: "I'd probably be one of the students the teacher would ask to be quiet."

Many shows about the son, Theo Huxtable, are clearly based on Cosby's childhood and his experiences with Ennis. Like the episode when Theo's grades are going down and he thinks he should just go out and become an ordinary worker. "Maybe I was meant to be a regular person," he says. "Maybe you should accept me and love me as I am because I'm your son."

The audience is hushed. Cosby is touched by the boy's sincerity. "Theo," he begins, the words suddenly gathering steam, "that's the *dumbest* thing I've ever heard in my whole *life!*" He then teaches him the importance of money and a job with a future. But in other episodes, the lesson has to be relearned. In one, Theo is behaving like other yuppy-influenced kids: He's gone out and bought a ninety-five-dollar "status" shirt. And it takes a half hour for him to see that status comes from inside.

The real-life Cosby kids have had to learn the same lesson, and it was difficult when they'd see Bill pick up car number fifteen, or go out to an auction to buy a $125,000 antique chair or a $95,000 set of Tiffany flatware. But Cos has taught them what value is all about, in both material things and intangibles. They know they'll inherit a lot of money when they grow up—Cosby's yearly income has been estimated at between seven million and ten million dollars—but Cos is firm: They won't get it if they don't complete their education.

In one episode Cos intimated that it wouldn't take an A average to get all that gravy. When Theo gets a B-plus on a paper and worries that it's not good enough, his father says, "An A is just a grade. The important thing is that you applied yourself." With Theo, Bill's getting to use some of the father-and-son dialogue from his stand-up act. It must have been a kick for Cos to tell Theo what his dad told him for years: "I'm your father. I brought you into this world, I'll take you out of it."

Most episodes of the show involve questions of parental trust and communication. When Theo is accused of smoking marijuana and denies it, his father says, "You are some things, some good, some bad, but you are not a liar." Cos detests lying and excuse-making in children, and always tries to keep communication open and free of the negativity that breeds lies. As for his own kids' drug-free and scandal-free lives, he says it's as much a matter of luck as anything else, but education and communication *can* help.

Sometimes big problems on the set don't require big discussions. Lisa Bonet returned to the show for the second season wearing an entirely new hairstyle. She'd cut it short over the summer, slim on the sides and bushy over the forehead. This had *not* been cleared by NBC, and could have been a major disaster. Television viewers like their favorites to look familiar every week, almost to the point where they wear a "uniform" in every episode of the same color coordinates. "He's teasing me," Lisa says of Cos, "but his wife has short hair, so I think he likes it."

Sometimes there's a reversal. Instead of art imitating life and Cosby episodes being drawn from real experiences, things on the show have an impact on Bill's actual family. In one script Sondra was getting set for a sojourn in Paris. This was especially exciting to . . . Erika Cosby. "Hey Dad, how about sending your *real* daughter to France?" Cos thought for a moment and . . . *voilà*. The entire Cosby clan was set for a two-week summer vacation in Europe.

Of course, household communication can get comically strained at times. The dialogue in the Huxtable household is realistically humorous. Theo to his father:

"Dad, Denise is hogging the bathroom."

"Use the one downstairs."

"But that's the guest bathroom."

"Well, pretend you don't live here!"

When Heathcliff quizzes his daughter Vanessa, his wife joins in for a typical three-way family argument. He asks, "Did you practice the clarinet?" Vanessa, in all innocence, deadpans, "You didn't *make* me." In comes his wife, all exasperation: "Will you tell your daughter how important this is?" Cliff looks at her in amazement. "You planning on leaving town right away? The girl is standing right there! *You* tell her!"

Rarely does the show lapse into sitcom-style unbelievability—though in one episode an Oriental husband, after seeing a film on the birth of a baby, faints dead away every time Dr. Huxtable mentions "labor pains" or "the film."

More often the warm, natural humor flows, as Cliff tries to guess his birthday surprise, or his children try to find ways of wheedling a secret out of him. There are the never-ending feuds with the date-aged daughters. Cliff asks one: "How ugly is he? Who's his parole officer?" And when she's about to go out of the house in tight pants, he says, "No! Blood can't get up to your head!" When she dresses up in a trashy punk outfit, or when Theo wants to practice shaving his hairless face, Cos says nothing at all: He gives a deep, throaty gurgle of laughter, one of the newer weapons in his comedy arsenal.

At forty-eight, Cosby's face is more mobile and expressive than ever before, and some mild scenes around the dinner table or living room sofa are livened up by brow-furrowing scowls, worry-eyed perplexed looks, and blameless grins.

"He's not only a great comedian," says Phylicia Ayers-Allen, who plays his wife Clair, "he's a great actor." Lisa Bonet agrees: "Bill is real honest, and he goes out of his way to help us, critiquing and complimenting our work."

The relationship between Clair and Cliff Huxtable does mirror Cosby's life with Camille. One episode, about the couple trying to get away from their kids for a weekend, echoed the real-life joy Bill and Camille had when they spent Easter by themselves:

"Oh, that was juicy! That's a fine Easter, man. Or Passover or whatever it was. We were havin' a ball that weekend. It was quiet. We just stood in the room and said, 'Listen to this—this is the sound of our children not being here.' "

Cosby's TV wife is an independent woman. So is Camille. Cosby's encouraged her to go to graduate school, and even flying school. Cos is in good hands when his wife takes him flying, but the more he thinks about it, the more it brings out a bit of comical resentment: "I know my wife, and I get in the plane with her, but . . . she's sort of bossy . . . in the plane, you know, and she uses that to get me to do things that I would say no to. So it isn't fair the way she uses that plane. She'll get me up there and if there's a little turbulence she'll say, 'I'm the only one who knows what's going on up here and there's something I'd like to talk to you about.' And she really makes me believe she really doesn't mind going down in this thing."

Camille encouraged Bill during the tough phases of *The Cosby Show*'s development. "That lady has stood so solidly with me for all these years," he told Alex Haley. "Whenever the time comes when one of us needs the other's support, that support is there, and it's real because we love each other. And we'll say, 'Thanks a lot for that. I really needed it.' I don't come home at night expecting Camille to be there to rub my back, but I do try to be there to rub hers whenever she needs it. These are the things that make our marriage work."

The actress who plays Camille's on-screen counterpart has many of Camille's attributes. Phylicia is a single mother, working hard to raise her young son properly. Like Camille, she's often described as cool, classy, and well-educated. Coincidentally, both women have fathers who are in the medical profession. Phylicia's mother is Vivian Ayers, a writer who was nominated for a Pulitzer Prize as the author of *Spice of Dawns*. One reason the show works in its portrayal of upper-middle-class blacks is because most of the principals *are* just that. Cos made it; so did the rest. And the joy of that reality shows.

"It's wonderful working with Bill because he's always looking out for everyone," Phylicia says. But he isn't the stern taskmaster or iron ruler all the time. "He's the most intelligent silly person I've ever met," she adds.

How can you be both intelligent and silly? Well, one day on the set young Keshia had to do a leap into the air. The little girl was terrified. When she finally summoned the courage to try the jump, she tumbled over and smacked her head against the floor.

People ran forward as the girl began to cry, but it was wise Cos who got her attention. When he saw that she was all right, he flung himself down on the floor and pretended that he too had gotten hurt just by deliberately falling down. His tantrum of woeful cries got the girl giggling gleefully.

"He loves watching kids," his TV wife says. "That's why this series works, because it's based on human behavior, not one-liners. There's so much love in it, so much truth in it, there's so much heart in the writing, directing, and the performance. It seems people enjoy seeing the best part of themselves in it."

She appears to be as aware as Cosby is of the importance of the image they're projecting: "I think Bill and I are great role models as far as our TV professions are concerned. Kids learn by example and I think we're very good ones."

Camille is usually at the tapings. The studio audience recognizes her —who else would Cos suddenly walk off the stage to talk to and kiss— but she has also appeared, indirectly, in front of a national audience.

When Bill hosted a special on the reopening of the Apollo Theater in the spring of 1985, he wore a photo T-shirt with a picture of her on it and the words CAMILLE'S HUSBAND. Every day he wears a bracelet with those very same words on it. Sometimes on the show it can be spotted, glinting off his right wrist.

One of the most positive things about the Apollo special was that Cosby was considered the perfect choice to oversee all the different black styles from gospel to disco-funk to tap dance. That night it seemed as though people were willing to accept all the variations in black entertainment without finding one or the other demeaning or bad for the image.

Perhaps in comedy, too, there is room for all types of black comics—mirroring all types of black people. Some may talk and act like Redd Foxx, others like Bill Cosby. The black experience and the truth in comedy are reflected in all the comics—from the jolly, funky, and footloose (Markham, Murphy, and Wilson) to the satiric, salty, and soulful (Gregory, Pryor, and Mabley).

The Cosby Show received eight Emmy nominations for the first season. Of course, Bill wasn't up for one. Along with Michael Landon, he felt he'd won enough awards and it was time to let someone else benefit from the honor. But his TV wife, Phylicia Ayers-Allen, was nominated for best actress in a comedy series. Meanwhile her sister, Debbie Allen, was nominated for best actress in a dramatic series for her work in *Fame*.

It didn't take long for all three networks to try for Emmy-winning, top-rated sitcoms using Cosby's formula. But the watered down versions that premiered in the fall of 1985 missed the most important ingredient: Bill Cosby. Cosby, both in front of and behind the camera, *made* his show work.

Flip Wilson, evidently fed up with Cosby comparisons even before the season began, banged the drum for his show, *Charlie & Company* by knocking Cos: "Cosby's family is bourgeois; we're an average black family. . . . I don't think Cosby has as much depth as I do." Flip's show hit the depths of the ratings cellar. The season's other "warm, family-oriented" sitcoms, *227* and *Growing Pains,* fared only slightly better. *The Cosby Show* retained its #1 position for the new year.

When the show resumed production for its second season, Cosby was not about to coast, even with the nation's number one show. On August 9, the day of the first taping of the season, Cosby stepped out between scenes to address the audience. "Ladies and gentlemen," he began

slowly and soberly, "on behalf of the cast . . . the crew . . . the producers . . . the director . . . the assistants. We are very happy to be
back.

"The second season means an awful lot to us, especially because of
where we are in the ratings. We didn't know where we would be last
year. However, this does not give us any particular, uh, rest spot. We
have to continue to give you the quality that you ask for." The audience
was hushed by the dead seriousness of Cosby's measured speech. "We
certainly hope *this* particular show will give you a feeling that *The
Cosby Show* is going to be as good, perhaps even better than last year.
This episode of course is about the first day of school. I'm sure all of
you can identify with these children having a problem getting out of
bed. So if anyone asks about *The Cosby Show* this year, you just tell 'em
we're working even *harder,* to make this the kind of program that you
can sit with your children, with your parents, and enjoy."

The slow cadence, the earnest expression on Bill's face did not
change. "And then before you go to bed," he continued, "have a good
discussion about how much you love each other, and understand and
get along with each other . . . regardless of the fact that they're your
parents"—the audience began to giggle—"or your children." The audience continued to laugh and applaud.

"You can get a good discussion from both sides. Thank you very
much; we will try and keep you entertained during the breaks." Cosby
turned around and noticed Tempestt Bledsoe entering the living room
set, dressed in a conspicuously fancy dress. Cos smirked and said, "This
year you will notice our own actress here, Tempestt Bledsoe, carrying
on with some fashion." The girl smiled as the audience laughed. Cos,
his voice low in conspiratorial glee, added, "And this year we have
something new with Vanessa, her character. The breast fairies have
arrived! And she doesn't know where she's going or what she's doing,
she just knows she has certain feelings about her body and herself, and
this will be a good year . . ."

Someone called for Bill, the cameras got ready, and the audience
burst into applause before hushing themselves in anticipation of the
funny scenes to follow.

NBC had good reason to anticipate the second season, too. In addition to Cosby's number one ratings, a TVQ survey done for networks
and ad agencies rated Cos the number one star in the land in terms of
"familiarity and likability." In fact, he had the highest ratings in the
twenty years of the survey, far outdistancing second-place Clint East-

wood, third-place Alan Alda, and other also-rans like Bob Hope, Tom Selleck, Paul Newman, and Carol Burnett. Naturally, with news like this, NBC upped the rates for *Cosby Show* commercials. Even to Jell-O, one of the show's first sponsors. When the show first arrived, NBC was charging $110,000 for a thirty-second spot. Now the price is up to $200,000, making it one of the most expensive shows on the air (*60 Minutes* was a leader at $190,000).

Each episode costs $450,000 to produce.

Cos got raves from everybody. Who did Howard Cosell deem just about the only one who could take his place on *Monday Night Football?* "That's right, Bill Cosby," raved the normally crusty Cosell. "He'd really shake things up, make people notice . . . he knows what he's talking about. . . . he's a brilliant communicator . . . witty, knowledgeable and vastly entertaining."

Professionally, Cos has the best of both worlds—ten weeks a year guaranteed at Las Vegas and Atlantic City, and *The Cosby Show.* He says of his work: "This series is for me a love affair for all the years that I've been a well-paid entertainer. It's my way to say to the people who have enjoyed my work, 'I can do this, and here is a form of entertainment that I hope you will all feel good about.' I feel as though the love I have to give to people is appreciated. I just want to give more and more and more."

Personally, Cosby has a happy home, and he has Camille: "My life now is a very, very happy one. It's a happiness of being deeply connected, of knowing that there is someone I can trust completely, and that the one I trust is the one I love. I also know that the one *she* loves is definitely one she can trust. It is immeasurable, the wisdom she has given me. With her strength and help, I can only become better . . . and I want to . . . because I want her to be proud of me."

Cosby has reason to feel a sense of pride in all he has accomplished, in all the laughter and love and understanding he has brought to audiences with his work. The involvement between audience and artist is mutual. He is one of America's most beloved entertainers. "As for involvement," Cosby says, "I'm emotionally involved with *life.*"

Spoken Word Comedy Albums

Bill Cosby Is a Very Funny Fellow . . . Right! (Warner Bros. W 1518)
Featuring Bill's two key early bits, "Noah and the Ark" and "Karate." Plus: "A Nut in Every Car," "Toss of the Coin," "Little Tiny Hairs," "Superman," "Hoof and Mouth," "Greasy Kid Stuff," "The Difference Between Men and Women," "The Pep Talk." Recorded at the Bitter End.

I Started Out as a Child (Warner Bros. W 1567)
Bill's first childhood reminiscences appear on this one: "Sneakers," "Street Football," "The Water Bottle," "Christmas Time," "The Giant." An embryonic, minute-long version of "TV Football" is included, along with some mildly sick/hip humor reflecting the early-sixties era ("Ralph Jameson," "Medic," "Rigor Mortis," "Seattle"), bits on "The Lone Ranger" and "The Wolfman," his classic bit about a lisping saber-toothed tiger and his nemesis, "The Neanderthal Man." Plus "Oops!," "My Pet Rhinoceros." Recorded at Mr. Kelly's in Chicago.

Why Is There Air? (Warner Bros. W 1606)
The breakthrough album coming in at the same time as *I Spy,* offering the brilliant football routine "Hofstra," taking Midol for "The Toothache," an extended routine on "Kindergarten," a quick bit on jock straps, "Personal Hygiene," plus "Shop," "Baby," "Driving in San Francisco," "$75 Car" (an auto that manages to go down hills sideways, with a sleepy Cos at the wheel). Recorded at the Flamingo Hotel, Las Vegas.

Wonderfulness (Warner Bros. W 1634)
Two extended routines, each more than twelve minutes long, build to hysterical climaxes of comedy. There's Bill spreading Jell-O on the floor to battle the giant menace throbbing on the radio, "The Chicken Heart," and the famous story about hospitals, ice cream and "Tonsils." Plus a query on why adults would put something as dangerous as monkey bars into "The Playground," "Lumps" lurking in Cream of Wheat,

"Go-Carts," "Shop," "Special Class," and a Sheldon Leonard anecdote about vacationing at "Niagara Falls." Recorded at Harrah's, Lake Tahoe.

Revenge (Warner Bros. WS 1691)

Vivid stories of Cosby's childhood gang predominate. The boys shiver through a horror movie only to have to go home over the "9th Street Bridge." Fat Albert is introduced as the two-thousand-pounder who makes the ground shake when he plays "Buck Buck." The most classic routine of all is the title cut, Bill with a snowball in his icebox, in midsummer, waiting to get "Revenge" against Junior Barnes, who hit him in the face with a slushball the previous winter. Plus "Two Daughters," "Two Brothers," "The Tank," "Smoking," "Wives," "Cool Covers," "Planes." Recorded at Harrah's, Lake Tahoe.

To Russell My Brother Whom I Slept With (Warner Bros. WS 1734)

The title cut is a twenty-six-minute uncut, unedited slice of comic life —the tale of two brothers battling Dad at bedtime. When they jump on the bed and break it, and Dad storms in, they've got a panicky excuse: "Some man came in here, started jumpin' on the bed, Dad . . . he came in through the window . . . we told him you better cut it out . . . and he broke it and ran out the window laughin'." Bill talks about his young daughters ("The Losers") and "Baseball," "Conflict," "The Apple." Recorded in Cleveland, 1968.

200 MPH (Warner Bros. WS 1757)

Cos talks about gifts on "Mother's Day" and "Father's Day," stockings in the sink and other problems with "The Wife," and recalls his "Grandfather," who taught him to smoke cigars "to keep the worms away." Plus "Dogs and Cats," and the title cut, an informal twenty-two-minute rap about sports-car driving, complete with audience participation and jeers for Volkswagen owners. Recorded at Harrah's, Lake Tahoe.

It's True, It's True (Warner Bros. WS 1770)

An early crossover album of kid stuff ("Ants Are Cool," "Shoelaces," "Mr. Ike and the Neighborhood TV Set") with adult stuff ("It's the Women's Fault," "Helicopters," "The American Gambler," "Spanish Fly"). On "Burlesque Shows" he wonders "why men go into a place and watch a lady take her clothes off. That's sick. If you're hungry, you don't go watch a guy cook a steak. You move away from it!" Cos wings it for fourteen minutes talking about his *I Spy* travels in "Foreign Countries." Does Japan really have nude bathing? "It's true," Cos squeals. "It's true!"

8:15 12:15 (Tetragrammaton TD-5100)

His only double-album set. Cosby is heard in true Vegas form, rapping with ringsiders, ad-libbing and kibitzing, talking about gambling and how dumb golf is ("You got the ball. You had it right there. Then . . . you hit it away! And then . . . you go and walk after it again! It's a dumb game!"). At eighty minutes flowing over four sides, it confused fans expecting tight mini-routines. It was his only release on the ill-fated label he co-owned.

Bill Cosby: Sports (UNI 73066; MCA 552)

Bill's debut album for Uni Records (the label is now known as MCA Records) was totally sports-oriented, with routines on: "Football," "Baseball," "Track and Field," "Mile Relay," "Bill Cosby Goes to a Football Game," "High Jump."

Live at Madison Square Garden (UNI 73082)

One of the best of the Uni releases. Cos talks about a frustrating encounter with a wily, aged handball player ("Handball at the Y") and tells an anecdote about one of his most embarrassing foot-in-mouth moments ("Bill Visits Ray Charles"). He talks about the birth of "His First Baby" ("If the baby's born, what do you keep and waddya throw away?"). Plus "Bill Takes His Daughter to the Zoo," "Ennis and His Two Sisters," "Animal Stories," "The Story of the Chicken."

When I Was a Kid (UNI 73100; MCA 169)

A mild album of remembrances of things past, including an extended routine about going to see "Buck Jones," a cowboy hero so cool he never got his hat knocked off in a fight. Plus: "Hernia," "Snakes and Alligators," "My Boy Scout Troop," "My Brother Russell," "My Father," "Dogs," "Frogs."

For Adults Only (UNI 73112; MCA 553)

A crossover LP in many ways, including the first extended humor of parent versus child instead of child versus parent, it offers slightly risqué humor ("Las Vegas: Mirror Over My Bed," "Wallie Wallie"), husband-wife comedy ("Why Beat on Your Wife," "Bill Cosby Fights Back," "Be Good to Your Wives," "Masculinity at Its Finest"), plus observations on "Bill's Two Daughters," "The Cost of an Egg."

Inside the Mind of Bill Cosby (UNI 73139; MCA 554)

Released in 1972 during his variety show run, this mild LP offers lectures on "The Invention of Basketball" and the effect of chitlins on "The Lower Tract": "That's pig intestines! That includes the lower tract—ain't no food down in that area. Chitlins . . . I think somebody misspelled that word." Plus: "Slow Class," "Bedroom Slippers," "Survival," "Ennis's Toilet," "Bill's Marriage," "Froofie the Dog," "Sulphur Fumes," "Football."

Fat Albert (MCA 333)

Having risen from a supporting role in previous albums (beginning with "Buck Buck" on *Revenge*) to the star of his own TV cartoon, Cosby's hefty comedy favorite is the main attraction of this album, released in 1973.

My Father Confused Me, What Must I Do? (Capitol ST-11590)

An excellent comeback album. Cos scores with vivid stories about parental discipline ("My Father Confused Me," "Mothers Enunciate," "The FCC and Mothers," "Mothers Will Hit You for Nothing"), plus "The English Language," "Henry Kissinger," "UFO," "The Glazed Donut Monster," "Fathers Are the Funniest People," "Marriage and Duties," "New Husbands Kill Things," "The Lizard and the Mouse," "Dudes on Dope," "The Dentist." Recorded in 1977.

Bill's Best Friend (Capitol ST-11731)

Roland Johnson could turn his eyelids inside out and curse cool ("Gad dang!") and is the hero of the mild nine-minute "Roland and the Rollercoaster." Cos does six minutes of sound effects ("Cars"), observes how exhausting it is to snort coke and smoke pot ("Illegal Drugs"), and amazes his date with bleeding eyes and a runny nose from "Chinese Mustard." Plus: "Parents and Grandparents," "Famous People," "Let's Make a Deal," "Frisbees," "People Who Drink," "Puberty." Recorded in 1978.

Bill Cosby Himself (Motown ML 6026)

The "original soundtrack" from his live-performance movie. Bill talks about domestic problems with the kids ranging from morning rituals ("Chocolate Cake for Breakfast") to an evening's hysteria as three of them battle over taking a shower ("Same Thing Happens Every Night"). Classics are here, too: "The Dentist," "Grandparents," "Kill the Boy," "Brain Damage," "Natural Childbirth."

Comedy Compilations

Warner Bros. has issued two *Best of Bill Cosby* albums. The first offers: "Noah and the Ark," "Revenge," "Lone Ranger," "Old Weird Harold [9th Street Bridge]," "Driving in San Francisco," "The Apple," "Babies," "Water Bottle," "Street Football," "Buck Buck." The second has: "Two Daughters," "Toss of the Coin," "Conflict," "Dogs and Cats," "Smoking," "Shop," "Karate," "Oops," "The Apple," "Hofstra."

MCA has a two-record set culled from his Uni/MCA years, called *Bill.* It has: "Handball at the Y," "Froofie the Dog," "Survival," "Fernet Branca," "Wallie Wallie," "My Dad's Car," "The Lower Tract," "Be Good to Your Wives," "Bill Cosby Fights Back," "Buck Jones," "Bill Cosby's First Baby," "Basketball," "Fat Albert's Car," "Snakes and Alligators," "Track and Field," "Ennis's Toilet," "Brother Russell," "Masculinity at Its Finest."

Cosby Music Albums

Silver Throat Sings (Warner Bros. 1709)

The first of his "rocking soul" albums. The cuts are mostly serious, with one cut written by Cosby ("Doncha Know") and another written by Moy-Wonder-Cosby ("Little Ole Man"). Other songs: "Mojo Workout," "I Got a Woman," "Place in the Sun," "Bright Lights Big

City," "Big Boss Man," "Hush Hush," "Baby What You Want Me to Do," "Tell Me You Love Me," "Aw Shucks Hush Your Mouth." Released in 1968.

Hooray for the Salvation Army Band (Warner 7 Arts 1728)

Humorously exaggerated treatments of soul classics ("Hold On! I'm Comin'," "Reach Out I'll Be There") and rock classics ("I Can't Get No Satisfaction," "Sgt. Pepper's Lonely Hearts Club Band") highlight this relaxed release. Cuts written or co-written by Cosby: "Funky North Philly," "Ursalena," "Time Brings About a Change," "Stop Look & Listen," "Hooray for the Salvation Army Band." Others: "Sunny," "I'm a Road Runner," "Get Out of My Life Woman."

Bill Cosby Presents Badfoot Brown and the Bunions Bradford Funeral and Marching Band (UNI 73080)

Temporarily retiring his vocal chords, Bill offered jazz jamming instead. The first side contains the fifteen-minute "Martin's Funeral," a musical interpretation of Bill's feelings attending services for Dr. Martin Luther King, Jr. Side two is a twenty-minute jam called "Hybish Shybish." Music composed by Bill Cosby. Released c. 1970.

Bill Cosby Presents Badfoot Brown and the Bunions Bradford Funeral and Marching Band (Sussex/Buddah SXBS 7024)

More jazz instrumental jams, including the upbeat cut "Bunions," the fifteen-minute "Abuse," and an almost haunting, melodious cut blending African percussion and sax riffs, "I Love You Camille." Cosby still isn't singing: the two cuts that have lyrics ("The Blues," "Mouth of the Fish") are sung by Stu Gardner. All selections written by Bill Cosby. Released in 1972.

At Last Bill Cosby Really Sings (Partee PBS 2405)

True to the title, sizzling instrumentals and vocals mostly sung in Bill's natural low baritone rather than straining for the high notes. Cuts written by Bill Cosby and Stu Gardner: "It's Strange," "Dance of the Frozen Lion," "Take Your Time," "Train to Memphis," "Kiss Me," "No One Can Love the Way You Do." Cut written by Bill Cosby: "Dedicated to Phyliss." Others: "Special Lady Sweetness," "Put Love in Its Proper Place." Recorded in 1974.

Bill Cosby Is Not Himself These Days, Rat Own, Rat Own, Rat Own (Capitol ST 11530)

A breakthrough album of cuts that mostly satirize popular R&B and funk stars. Cuts written by Bill Cosby and Stu Gardner: "Yes, Yes, Yes," "Chick on the Side," "I Luv Myself Better Than I Luv Myself," "Do It to Me," "Ben," "You're Driving Me Crazy," "Garbage Truck Lady," "Luv Is." Cut written by Cosby, Gardner, and Steve Lansbury: "Shift Down." Recorded in 1976.

Disco Bill (Capitol ST 11683)

The follow-up album offering more of the same, but with a little more of Bill's own style of funny funk coming through. Cut written by Bill Cosby: "A Nasty Birthday." Cuts written by Bill Cosby and Stu Gardner: "A Simple Love Affair," "What Ya Think 'bout Lickin' My Chicken," "Rudy," "Boogie on Your Face," "That's How I Met Your Mother," "What's in a Slang," "Section #9." Cut written by Cosby-Gardner-Mays: "Happy Birthday Momma." Plus: "One Two Three."

Other Cosby Recordings and Writings

In addition to his own comedy and music albums, Cosby appears on *Diana: The Original TV Soundtrack* (Motown) as a guest on Diana Ross's 1971 special. His 1972 appearance before of *The Congressional Black Caucus* was released on Motown's documentary label, Black Forum.

For the original cast album of *The Electric Company* (Warner Bros.), he talk-sings two funky humor cuts, "Downright Uptight" ("You dragged me down, baby, I'm downright uptight 'cause of you") and "Jelly Belly" ("nice and fat—where it's at!"). He also teaches kids about "Double E." For *Bill Cosby Talks to Kids about Drugs* (MCA) he offers advice and songs.

Cosby's involvement in jazz included producing and arranging an album called *For the Cos of Jazz* (Capitol) featuring the First Cousins Jazz Ensemble.

He wrote the original liner notes for 1972's *Charles Mingus and Friends* and is credited with writing the liner notes for Joan Rivers's first album, *Mr. Phyllis.*

As an author, Bill Cosby has two volumes to his credit: *Fat Albert's Survival Kit* (Windmill Books) and *Bill Cosby's Personal Guide to Tennis Power* (Random House). He's written pieces for a variety of publications, including *Playboy, Ebony,* and the *Chicago Daily News.*

Movies and Videocassettes

Man and Boy (1972; 98 min.) with Bill Cosby as Caleb, Gloria Foster as his wife, George Spell as his son. Including: Douglas Turner Ward, Yaphet Kotto, Henry Silva, Dub Taylor, Leif Erickson, John Anderson. A family western, the story of a father and son's adventures protecting their homestead and tracking down the man who stole their horse. Directed by E. W. Swackhamer. Screenplay by Harry Essex and Oscar Saul.

Hickey and Boggs (1972; 111 min.) with Bill Cosby as Al Hickey, Robert Culp as Frank Boggs, Rosalind Cash as Nyona Boggs. Including: Vincent Gardenia, Louis Moreno, Ron Henrique, Robert Mandan, and Lou Frizzell. Bill and Bob play a pair of rundown detectives trying to recover $400,000 in stolen money. Directed by Robert Culp. Screenplay by Walter Hill.

Uptown Saturday Night (1974; 104 min.) with Bill Cosby as Wardell Franklin, Sidney Poitier as Steve Jackson, Rosalind Cash as Sarah Jackson, Ketty Lester as Irma Franklin, Lee Chamberlin as Madame Zenobia, Calvin Lockhart as Silky Slim, Harry Belafonte as Geechie Dan. Including: Richard Pryor, Flip Wilson, Roscoe Lee Browne, Harold Nicholas. A factory worker and cab driver go after gangsters who made off with a wallet containing a fifty-thousand-dollar lottery ticket. Directed by Sidney Poitier. Screenplay by Richard Wesley.

Let's Do It Again (1975; 112 min.) with Bill Cosby as Bill Foster, Sidney Poitier as Clyde Williams, Lee Chamberlin as Dee Dee Williams, Denise Nicholas as Beth Foster, Calvin Lockhart as Biggie Smalls, John Amos as Kansas City Mack, Ossie Davis as Elder Johnson, Jimmie Walker as Bootney Farnsworth. Using hypnosis, two lodge brothers try to fix a fight and save their community center. Directed by Sidney Poitier. Screenplay by Richard Wesley.

Mother, Jugs and Speed (1976; 98 min.) with Bill Cosby as Mother Tucker, Raquel Welch as Jennifer "Jugs" Jurgens, Harvey Keitel as Speed, Allen Garfield as Harry Fishbine, L. Q. Jones as Davey, Larry Hagman as Murdoch, Milt Kamen as Barney. Including: Dick Butkus, Bruce Davison, Valerie Curtin, Bill Henderson, and Toni Basil. A *M*A*S*H* on wheels: life with a high-living ambulance squad. Directed by Peter Yates. Screenplay by Tom Mankiewicz.

A Piece of the Action (1977; 135 min.) with Bill Cosby as Dave Anderson, Sidney Poitier as Manny Durrell, James Earl Jones as Joshua Blake, Denise Nicholas as Lila French. Including Hope Clarke, Tracy Reed, Titos Vandis, Marc Lawrence, and Jason Evers. It takes two— Bill and Sidney—to help a social worker reach young street kids. Directed by Sidney Poitier. Screenplay by Charles Blackwell.

California Suite (1978; 103 min.) with Bill Cosby as Dr. Willis Panama, Richard Pryor as Dr. Chauncey Gump, Gloria Gifford as Lola Gump, Sheila Frazier as Bettina Panama. And starring in the film's other segments: Alan Alda, Jane Fonda, Walter Matthau, Elaine May, Maggie Smith, and Michael Caine. Two doctors encounter slapstick misfortunes and miseries; comedy relief for the problems of three other couples in a swanky hotel. Directed by Herbert Ross. Screenplay by Neil Simon.

The Devil and Max Devlin (1981; 96 min.) with Bill Cosby as Barney Satan, Elliott Gould as Max Devlin, Susan Anspach as Penny Hart, Adam Rich as Toby Hart, Julie Budd as Stella Summers, Sonny Shroyer as Big Billy Hunniker. Including: Charles Shamata, Deborah Baltzell, Ronnie Schell, Julie Parrish, and David Knell. A shifty landlord strikes a dying bargain: he can stay alive if he delivers three souls to the devil. Directed by Steven Hilliard Stern. Screenplay by Mary Rodgers.

Bill Cosby Himself (1983; 104 min.) Bill's solo performance film, written and directed by Bill Cosby himself.

Six of Bill Cosby's films have been released in videocassette versions, in both Beta and VHS. These include: *Uptown Saturday Night* (Warner Video), *Let's Do It Again* (Warner Video), *A Piece of the Action* (Warner Video), *California Suite* (Columbia Video), *The Devil and Max Devlin* (Disney Video), and *Bill Cosby Himself* (CBS/Fox Video).

Additionally, there are three volumes of cartoons available from Thorn/EMI Video based on the 1972 syndicated series *Fat Albert and the Cosby Kids.*

Walt Disney Video has also released several volumes of *Bill Cosby's Picture Pages.*

Grammy and Emmy Awards and Nominations

Emmy Awards for Television

1966   Outstanding Performance by an Actor in a Leading Role in a Dramatic Series, *I Spy* (NBC)

1967   Outstanding Performance by an Actor in a Leading Role in a Dramatic Series, *I Spy* (NBC)

1968   Outstanding Performance by an Actor in a Leading Role in a Dramatic Series, *I Spy* (NBC)

1969   "The Bill Cosby Special" (NBC)

1970   Nomination: Outstanding Musical or Variety Program, "The Second Bill Cosby Special" (NBC)

        Nomination: Outstanding Performance by an Actor in a Leading Role in a Comedy Series (NBC; he lost to William Windom)

Nomination: Outstanding New Series, *The Bill Cosby Show* (NBC) (lost to *Room 222*)

Nomination: Outstanding Comedy Series, *The Bill Cosby Show* (NBC) (lost to *My World and Welcome To It*)

1975   Nomination: Outstanding Individual Achievement in Children's Programming, "Highlights of the Ringling Brothers Barnum & Bailey Circus" (NBC) (lost to Elinor Bunin)

1981   Outstanding Individual Achievement in Children's Programming, "The Secret," episode of *The New Fat Albert Show* (CBS)

1985   Bill requested his name be removed from Best Actor consideration to give others a chance for exposure and honors. *The Cosby Show* itself won three Emmy Awards: Outstanding Comedy Series, Outstanding Writing in a Comedy Series, and Outstanding Directing in a Comedy Series.

Grammy Awards for Recordings
(All awards and nominations, unless otherwise noted, are for Best Comedy LP.)

1963   Nomination: *Bill Cosby Is a Very Funny Fellow . . . Right!* (lost to Allan Sherman)

1964   *I Started Out as a Child*

1965   *Why Is There Air?*

1966   *Wonderfulness*

1967   *Revenge*

1968   *To Russell My Brother Whom I Slept With*

1969   *Bill Cosby: Sports*

1970   Nomination: *Live at Madison Square Garden* (lost to Flip Wilson)

Nomination: *Grover Henson Feels Forgotten* (lost, in the Spoken Word category, to a recorded speech by Dr. Martin Luther King., Jr.)

1971   Best Recording for Children: *Bill Cosby Talks to Kids About Drugs*

Nomination: *When I Was a Kid* (lost to Lily Tomlin)

1972   Best Recording for Children: *The Electric Company*

1973   Nomination: *Fat Albert* (Lost to Cheech & Chong)

1976   Nomination: *Bill Cosby Is Not Himself These Days, Rat Own, Rat Own, Rat Own* (lost to Richard Pryor)

Television Series

I Spy (NBC, September 15, 1965–September 2, 1968). Bill Cosby as secret agent Alexander Scott, Robert Culp as secret agent Kelly Robinson.

The Bill Cosby Show (NBC, September 14, 1969–August 31, 1971). Bill Cosby as Chester "Chet" Kincaid, with supporting players appearing on an informal basis: Lillian Randolph (first year) and Beah Richards (second year) as Chet's mother, Fred Pinkard as Chet's father, Lee Weaver as Brian Kincaid, Olga James as Verna Kincaid, Sid McCoy as Principal Langford, Joyce Bulifant as guidance counselor Mrs. Peterson.

The Electric Company (PBS, 1971–1976). Guest stars included Bill Cosby, Rita Moreno, Lee Chamberlin, Jim Boyd, Morgan Freeman, Hattie Winston, Judy Graubart, Skip Hinnant, Irene Cara.

Fat Albert and the Cosby Kids (CBS, premiered September 9, 1972). Bill Cosby as himself, Fat Albert, and others. Additional voices by Jan Crawford, Gerald Edwards, Eric Suter, Erika Carroll, Michael Lee Gray, Keith Allen, Lane Vaux. Title changed in fall 1979 to *The New Fat Albert Show*.

The New Bill Cosby Show (CBS, September 11, 1972–May 7, 1973). Starring Bill Cosby. Regulars included Foster Brooks, the Donald McKayle Dancers, and Quincy Jones conducting the orchestra.

Cos (ABC, September 19, 1976–October 31, 1976). Starring Bill Cosby. Regulars included Buzzy Linhart, Jeff Altman, Timothy Thomerson, Marion Ramsey, Willie Bobo, Charlie Callas.

The Cosby Show (NBC, premiered September 20, 1984). Bill Cosby as Heathcliff Huxtable, Phylicia Ayers-Allen as his wife Clair, Sabrina Lebeauf as Sondra, Lisa Bonet as Denise, Malcolm Jamal Warner as Theo, Tempestt Bledsoe as Vanessa, Keshia Knight Pulliam as Rudy.

Index